Language Passport

Preparing for the IELTS Interview

Carolyn Catt

 LONGMAN

Photo credits:
Author: p 40 (b)(d)(f)
New Zealand Herald: p. 22 (left and top)
Rangiora Early Records Society: p. 40 (a)

Illustrations:
F.B.I./Donna Liddell

Addison Wesley Longman New Zealand Limited
46 Hillside Road, Auckland 10,
New Zealand

Associated companies throughout the world

© Addison Wesley Longman New Zealand Limited 1996
Reprinted 1999

ISBN 0582 87994 9

Produced by Addison Wesley Longman New Zealand Limited
Printed in Malaysia, GPS
Typeset in 10/12 Palatino

We use **paper from sustainable forestry**

Preface

Aims

The aim of *Language Passport* is to give students discussion practice on the sorts of topics that are likely to be included in the IELTS interview, and to equip them with the skills and functions that they may need to use in order to succeed in the interview.

Descriptions of the units

Each unit presents and practises a range of language structures and vocabulary items relevant to the topics, functions and skills of that unit. Accompanying pronunciation exercises focus on the suitable word stress, sentence stress and intonation patterns of the presented structures and vocabulary items.

Units 2–8 open with 'Revision exercises' which enable language functions, skills and vocabulary covered in the previous unit to be recycled in new contexts. (The revision exercises may also incorporate work in preparation for the coming unit's language foci.) This carrying over of spoken fluency practice into later lessons is an important feature, as repeated practice on different occasions – as provided by the homework and subsequent classroom work – aids memory and learning.

The recycling of language and skills is not limited to these homework and revision exercise tasks, but is also encouraged in a variety of activities within the body of the units so that, for example, work on asking questions is incorporated into units 1, 3, 4, 6, 7 and 8. While monitoring classroom work, teachers may, however, note the need for further conscious attention on the students' part to particular functions and skills, such as asking for repetition or dealing with difficult questions. This can be dealt with on an ad hoc basis by drawing the students' attention to the need for ongoing work in these areas during discussion and information exchange activities.

Activity types and interaction patterns

The format of the IELTS speaking test – a one-to-one interview – clearly influences the activity types and interaction patterns employed in *Language Passport*. However, limiting the activities to constant pairwork question and answer exercises would clearly result in repetitive and tedious lessons. Variety of focus and task type has therefore been incorporated, and recommended interaction patterns are given in the instructions for each exercise. The alternation of pair, group and whole-class work is designed to promote real communication through the exchange of information, and also to provide the stimulation that changes in interaction pattern and physical movement can bring to the English language classroom.

Taped interview excerpts

In addition to pronunciation practice work, the cassette tape includes a large number of simulated IELTS interview excerpts which illustrate a variety of important functions and skills. A complete example of an IELTS interview from start to finish is **not** included, as students might be tempted to try to learn it by heart, believing that this would help them in their own examination interview. This strategy would be most unwise, and it cannot be stressed too strongly that any examiner suspecting a candidate has memorised a passage or a 'speech' would be likely to change the topic to one that could not have been predicted and prepared – one that, as a result, the candidate may find very difficult to discuss. The aim of this book, therefore, is to encourage students to formulate their ideas about a range of topics that they may be asked to comment on, and to help them with the vocabulary and functional expressions they may use to express those ideas. It is not to encourage them to learn set responses.

Evaluation by peers

A number of tasks encourage students to evaluate each other's spoken work. It is important to ensure that students do not feel threatened by such tasks, but appreciate that the aim is to support rather than to judge each other. It is also important to ensure that students recognise peer evaluation as a means by which they can help each other, working together as a team to achieve their full potential. Conscious monitoring of other students' oral production can also assist students to become more aware of their own strengths and weaknesses, leading to greater autonomy in their language learning. Many tasks are designed, therefore, to foster cooperation and collaboration between students. In addition there are also team-based activities which serve to introduce a more competitive but light-hearted atmosphere at times.

Who is *Language Passport* suited to?

The book is intended, primarily, for groups of between 6 and 12 students who are intending to enter English-language medium colleges, polytechnics and universities. However, materials specifically designed for students who are taking the IELTS examination for New Zealand residence purposes have been provided where alternatives are required. At the same time, suggestions as to how to use the materials in monocultural and multicultural classes are incorporated, allowing for considerable flexibility of use, so that the book may be employed in schools operating within the students' own country as well as those in English-speaking countries.

Carolyn Catt

Contents

Map of the book

Unit	Title	Functions/skills	Topics	Relevance to IELTS interview sections
1	Introduction	• Asking questions • Greeting and introducing yourself • Saying goodbye	• Personal details	1, 3, 5 (2 and 4)
2	Static descriptions	• Describing things/giving general information • Dealing with vocabulary problems: - expressing non-comprehension - explaining unknown words • Asking for repetition	• Climate • Family • Language • Ethnic mix • Religion • Food • Festivals • Wedding ceremonies • Home towns	2 (all)
3	Questions and responses	• Asking questions • Responding to information	• Home towns • Student travelcard • Student cafeteria • Film club • Overseas students' support office • Scholarship • Birthday party • Student barbecue • Raffle ticket • Housing	3
4	Comparisons	• Comparing • Contrasting	• People • Roles of men and women • Countries • Education • Entertainment and hobbies • Crime • Politics • Marriage and divorce	2 (3 and 4)

Asking questions

Exercise 1

Work with a partner. Write down everything you and your partner know about the IELTS interview in the left-hand column below. In the right-hand column write questions about what you don't know and want to find out. (We have given you an example in each column.)

IELTS Interview

Things I know about the interview	Things I don't know about the interview (questions)
It tests my spoken English.	How long does it last?
....	....
....	....
....	....
....	....
....	....
....	....
....	....

Look at the questions you have written and check if you have a range of 'wh' questions – questions starting with the words 'who', 'what', 'how', 'where', 'why' and 'when'. If not, add more 'wh' questions using the complete range of 'wh' words.

Exercise 2

Divide the class into two groups: Group A and Group B. Group A should be made up of one student from each pair who worked together in Exercise 1. Group B should be made up of the other students from each pair. In your groups, compare what you wrote in the two columns above. Add any new information or any new questions. Work together to make sure your questions are grammatically correct.

Exercise 3

Work as a class. Each student should choose a different question from their Exercise 1 list. Write your questions on the board or on an overhead transparency so that all the class can look at them and check them for grammar mistakes. Try to help each other to correct any problems.

Exercise 4

Work in your two groups again. Group A students should read the text on page 103 of the Appendices. Group B students should read the text on page 110 of the Appendices. The texts are about the IELTS interview. Try to find the answers to your Exercise 1 questions and write them down.

Exercise 5

Work in pairs. Each pair should have one student from Group A and one student from Group B. Tell each other about the information you read that answered your questions in Exercise 1.

If you have any questions that you can't find the answers to, ask your teacher if he or she can answer them.

Exercise 6

Work individually. From the information you have read, match the following sections of the interview with the descriptions of what happens:

Section 1	talking on a familiar topic (about your background or your experiences)
Section 2	asking questions in a role play
Section 3	saying goodbye
Section 4	expressing plans and hopes for the future
Section 5	greeting and introducing yourself; providing personal information

Check your answers by looking at the texts on pages 103 and 110 of the Appendices.

Exercise 7

As a class, discuss where you would look to find the answer to the following question:

Which units of this book prepare you for the different sections of the IELTS interview?

 Now work individually and write your answers to the question here:

Section 1	Unit(s) ....
Section 2	Unit(s) ....
Section 3	Unit(s) ....
Section 4	Unit(s) ....
Section 5	Unit(s) ....

 Compare your answers as a class.

 ## Exercise 8

Work individually to answer the following questions:

1 Which section of the interview do you think you may find most difficult and why?

2 In what order would you put the following problems for you:
  a not knowing the vocabulary I need to use
  b not being able to give reasons for my opinions and ideas
  c having to pause to think about how to answer
  d not knowing the answer to the interviewer's question
  e not being able to understand some of the vocabulary the interviewer uses
  f not being able to hear what the interviewer says
  g not being clear about what the interviewer means

3 What other problems do you think you may have when speaking in the IELTS interview?

 Compare your answers in small groups and discuss what you can do to solve these problems.

 ## Exercise 9

Which units of the book deal with the different problems in Exercise 8(2)?

 ## Exercise 10

Look at the following sentences and decide if they are true or false. If they are false, correct them.

a A 'family name' is also known as a 'surname'.

b Your 'first language' is also called your 'father tongue'.

c An 'occupation' is a 'job'.

d An 'area of study' is the subject (e.g. business, tourism, computing) that someone studies.

e 'To take a test' means 'to pass a test'.

f To 'complete' something means to 'start' something.

g Your 'purpose' for doing something is also your 'reason' for doing something.

 Exercise 11

Work in pairs. Look at the following form about a student who is taking the IELTS examination (the form is similar to the Personal Details form that you have to complete when you register for the IELTS examination). Try to guess what information is missing. Write some of your guesses on the board.

1	Family name	Liu
2	First name	Jiang Mei

3 Address   34 Staines Road, Christchurch, New Zealand

4 Date of birth   5/4/72

5 Sex: F/M   Female

6 Nationality ......*Tywan Tiwan,*............

7 First language ......*Chines*.................

8 Occupation .....*Student*....................

9 Your purpose in taking the IELTS test:
- for further education —
- for work
- for personal reasons only

10 Your intended area of study:
- Physical sciences and related disciplines

- Biological sciences and related disciplines
- Humanities and social sciences and related disciplines
- General, industrial or vocational training, or upper secondary school programmes

11 Name of college/university/institution
you are applying to enter (if known) ....

12 Level of education you have completed:
- Secondary up to 16 years
- Secondary 16–19 years
- Degree or equivalent
- Post-graduate

13 Number of years you have studied English ....

Tapescript 1

Listen to the tape recording of the student talking to the IELTS examination organiser. The student has come to register for the IELTS exam, but she has lost her glasses, so the exam organiser is completing the form for her. As you listen, fill in the missing information on the form.

Compare the information that you heard on the tape with your guessed predictions. Did anyone in the class guess correctly?

Exercise 12

Work with a new partner. Write the questions you think the exam organiser asked on the tape for the following points of information from the form.

Point 6	....
Point 7	....
Point 8	....
Point 9	....
Point 11	....
Point 13	....

Listen to the tape and check your ideas. One student in each pair should listen for the questions for points 6, 8, and 11. The other student should listen for numbers 7, 9 and 13.

Exercise 13

Tapescript 2

Listen to the tape recording of the 6 questions from Exercise 12 and mark the main stresses in the questions. We have done the first one for you:

- Where are you **from**?
- Is your mother tongue Chinese?
- What do you do?
- Are you taking the IELTS test for further education, for work purposes or for personal reasons?
- Which institution are you applying to?
- How long have you been studying English?

Listen to the tape again and imitate the intonation and stress used.

Exercise 14

Work in pairs. Look at the following questions and mark where you think the main stress occurs.

a What's your surname?

b What's your first name?

c Can you give me your address, please?

d When were you born?

e Could you tell me what subject you are going to study?

f What level of education have you completed?

Tapescript 3

Listen to the tape to check your answers. Listen to the tape again and imitate the intonation and stress used.

Exercise 15

Each student in the class should choose a different question from Exercise 13 or Exercise 14. Mingle with all the other students and ask everyone your question. Make notes of their answers on your paper.

Summarise your findings and report them back to the class, e.g.

- Most students were born in the 1970s.
- Everyone has completed secondary school.
- Only two people are applying to the same institution.

Exercise 16

Work in pairs. Take it in turns to practise asking and answering the questions from Exercises 13 and 14.

Work with a new partner. Ask your partner questions and complete the form below from their answers. Try to ask for the information in a different order from the way it appears on the form and ask the questions from memory (do NOT look back at Exercises 13 or 14).

1 Family name ....

2 First name ....

3 Address ....

4 Date of birth ....

5 Sex: F/M ....

6 Nationality ....

7 First language ....

8 Occupation ....

9 Your purpose in taking the IELTS test:
   • for further education
   • for work
   • for personal reasons only

10 Your intended area of study:
   • Physical sciences and related disciplines
   • Biological sciences and related disciplines
   • Humanities and social sciences and related disciplines
   • General, industrial or vocational training, or upper secondary school

11 Name of college/university/institution you are applying to enter (if known)

   ....

12 Level of education you have completed:
- Secondary up to 16 years
- Secondary 16–19 years
- Degree or equivalent
- Post-graduate

13 Number of years you have studied English ....

Exercise 17

Work in small groups. Discuss what you remember about:

a what happens in Section 1 of the interview

b how long Section 1 lasts.

Look back at the texts on pages 103 and 110 of the Appendices to check your ideas.

Exercise 18

In the IELTS interview, the interviewer probably won't ask you questions to find out the information on the Personal Details form, because your completed Personal Data form will be in front of them. The interviewer will probably just check the information with a **comment**. But he or she may then ask **further questions** related to the information, e.g. for points 1 and 2 on the form, the interviewer may say:

Interviewer: Please say your name in full for me, would you. **[comment]**

Interviewee: Yes. It's Liu Jiang Mei.

Interviewer: And what would you like me to call you? **[further question]**

Match the following comments and questions together and decide in what order you think they occur in the interview. Number them according to their order.

Comments

- You're taking this IELTS exam to go on to further studies, I see.
- According to your form, you live in Staines Road here in Christchurch.
- And you're from Taiwan.
- Your first language is Chinese, of course.

- And it says here that you're a student.
- You say you're intending to study on a vocational training course.

Further questions
- Studying English, you mean?
- Is that an undergraduate or a postgraduate course?
- Whereabouts in Taiwan?
- What particular field?
- Do you speak any other languages?
- In a house or a flat?

Tapescript 4
Check your ideas by listening to the tape.

Exercise 19

Work in pairs. Work with the student who you interviewed in Exercise 16. Go through the Personal Details form making **comments** and asking **further questions** about the different items of information under points 1, 2, 3, 6, 7, 8, 9 and 10 on the form. You can use the ideas from Exercise 18 above.

Exercise 20

Fill in the form below about yourself.

1 Family name ....U. Jan me (May)...................

2 First name ....\May\...........................

3 Address ....Stains road. flat. Shoring. Tiwa.........

4 Date of birth ....

5 Sex: F/M ....F.............................

6 Nationality ....Tiwainies.................

7 First language ......Chines.....................

8 Occupation ....Tursion. lintin Univ..............

9   Your purpose in taking the IELTS test:
  • for further education
  • for work
  • for personal reasons only

10   Your intended area of study:
  • Physical sciences and related disciplines
  • Biological sciences and related disciplines
  • Humanities and social sciences and related disciplines
  • General, industrial or vocational training, or upper secondary school programmes

11   Name of college/university/institution you are applying to enter (if known)

  ....

12   Level of education you have completed:
  • Secondary up to 16 years
  • Secondary 16–19 years
  • Degree or equivalent
  • Post-graduate

13   Number of years you have studied English ....

Exercise 21

Exchange books with another student who you have not worked with so far in this lesson. Look at the completed form for Exercise 20 in your partner's book and decide on **comments** and **further related questions** you could make about the different points of information on the form.

  Now interview your partner using suitable comments and further questions but do NOT look back at Exercise 18 this time.

Greeting, introducing yourself and saying goodbye

Exercise 22

Check as a class if you remember:

a what happens in Section 5 of the interview

b how long Section 5 lasts.

Look at the texts on pages 103 and 110 of the Appendices to check your ideas.

 Exercise 23

Work individually. Look at the phrases below. Would the interviewer say these phrases in Section 5 of the interview or at the very beginning of Section 1? Write the number of the Section (1 or 5) next to each phrase.

- It's been nice meeting you. Goodbye.
- Hello, come on in.
- I see. Well, I think we'll end the interview there. So, I wish you luck with your plans…
- Yes, please. And take a seat.
- Well, I imagine you'll be feeling more relaxed now that you've finished the IELTS examination.
- My name's Susan and I'm your interviewer for today.
- And are you on holiday now?

 Tapescript 5

Listen to the tape to check your ideas and put the phrases in the correct order.

 Exercise 24

Work in pairs. Discuss what responses **you** would make to the interviewer's questions and comments below:

Section 1

Interviewer:	Hello, come on in.
Interviewee:	....
Interviewer:	My name's Susan and I'm your interviewer for today.
Interviewee:	....

Section 5

Interviewer:	I see. Well, I think we'll end the interview there. So, I wish you luck with your plans.
Interviewee:	....
Interviewer:	And are you on holiday now?
Interviewee:	....
Interviewer:	Well, I imagine you'll be feeling more relaxed now that you've finished the IELTS examination.
Interviewee:	....
Interviewer:	It's been nice meeting you, then. Goodbye.
Interviewee:	....

Work with a new partner and practise your responses.

Exercise 25: Role play

Divide the class into two groups:
- Group A are interviewers, each sitting behind an interview desk.
- Group B are interviewees.

The interviewees should take their Personal Details forms from Exercise 20 and give them to an interviewer. When the interviewers are ready, the interviewer and interviewee act out Sections 1 and 5 of the IELTS Speaking test. During the interview, remember to:

a start Section 1 with suitable greetings

b continue Section 1 with **comments** and then **further questions** about the information on the Personal Details form

c move to Section 5 when you have finished making **comments** and **further questions** from Section 1; use suitable farewells.

When you have finished, the interviewee should take his or her book to a new interviewer and act out Sections 1 and 5 again.

Change over so that Group B are the interviewers and Group A are the interviewees. Do the role play again.

Homework

Divide the class into two groups. Group A should look at the instructions on page 104 of the Appendices. Group B should look at the instructions on page 111.

Unit 2
Static descriptions

Revision

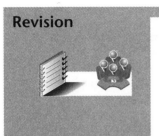

Work in the two groups you made for the Homework task at the end of Unit 1. In your groups, compare the questions you wrote for homework and choose the 10 best questions to ask the other group to answer.

When everyone is ready, read out your questions to the other group. Give them points for each correct answer. Find out which team has won.

Functions and topics in Section 2

Exercise 1

In Section 2 of the IELTS interview the interviewer may ask you to talk on a variety of **topics** and to use different **functions**. As a class, try to remember what **topics** were mentioned in the reading texts for Exercise 4 in Unit 1 of this book. Write your answers here:

List of topics for Section 2

Look at the texts on pages 103 and 110 of the Appendices to check your answers. If you missed any topics, add them to your list above.

Exercise 2

Again as a class, try to remember what **functions** were mentioned in the same texts (for Section 2 of the interview). **Functions** are such things as describing, apologising, complaining, giving advice, suggesting, inviting, etc. – in other words, things you use language to express. Can you remember any **functions** that you may be asked to express in Section 2 of the test? Write your answers here:

List of functions for Section 2

```
.......................................................................................................
.......................................................................................................
.......................................................................................................
```

Look at the texts on pages 103 and 110 of the Appendices to check your answers. If you missed any functions, add them to your list.

 Exercise 3

As a class, discuss where you would look to find the answer to the following question:

Which of the topics and functions you identified in Exercises 1 and 2 above are covered in this unit?

 Now work individually and write your answers to the question here:

Topics:	....
Functions:	....

Compare your answers as a class.

 Exercise 4

Work in pairs to answer the following questions:

1 What tense(s) do you think you will use most when describing things and giving general information about the topics in this unit?

2 Which units of this book deal with the other functions you may need to express in Section 2 of the IELTS speaking test, i.e.
   • Comparing and contrasting
   • Expressing desire to do something
   • Expressing likes and dislikes
   • Expressing interest in something
   • Expressing preferences
   • Describing a sequence of events
   • Expressing opinions
   • Giving reasons

3 What other functions are covered in this unit?

Describing things

Climate
Exercise 5

Work in small groups. Organise the following vocabulary into categories.

extreme	snow	wet	humid	cold	winter	sunny
cloudy	spring	alpine	sub-tropical	dry	summer	rain
monsoon	hot	autumn	sunshine	clouds	dry	equatorial
warm	moderate	tropical	cool	mild	winds	dull

Compare your ideas with other students' ideas. Did they have the same categories as you or not?

Exercise 6

Tapescript 6
Listen to the tape of someone talking about the climate in their country. As you listen:

a underline any of the vocabulary items in Exercise 5 that you hear on the tape

b decide if the climate the student is describing is similar to the climate in your country or city.

Check your answers as a class.

Exercise 7

Work in pairs. Fill in the gaps in the tapescript below.

I suppose my country .... a fairly moderate ....

There .... four distinct seasons: spring, summer, autumn and

winter. The winter .... very cold – it's generally quite mild; the

temperatures rarely .... below five degrees centigrade. But

.... also quite wet .... winter and very cloudy
and dull. Cold winds .... across the country ....
the north quite .... in spring and autumn, but the summer is
generally warm, ... temperatures around, say, 20 to 26 degrees
centigrade and .... of sunshine. Even so, when it rains in
summer the temperatures can .... to a cool 15 degrees, but they
.... quickly again when the clouds ....

 Listen to the tape again to check your answers.

 ### Exercise 8

Work individually. Use as many of the items of vocabulary as you
can to write a description of the climate in your country. Write your
description clearly so that other students can read it.
- If you are in a multicultural class, do not write the name of your
  country in your description. When you have finished, put all the
  descriptions on the walls round the class and then walk round to
  try and decide which country each description is about.
- If you are in a monocultural class, discuss what you have written
  with another student and find out if they wrote the same as you.
  If not, was it because you come from cities with very different
  climates, or was it because you have different ideas about your
  country?

 ### Exercise 9

Work individually. Imagine the perfect climate for you and put
a circle round the vocabulary in Exercise 5 that you could use
to describe that climate. In small groups, tell each other about
your 'perfect climate' using the vocabulary you circled in
Exercise 5. Check if any other students have the same
'perfect climate' as you.

Describing things

Family
Exercise 10

Work in small groups. Tell your partners about your family. Talk about any family members who live in your house in your home country. You can talk about the following subjects:
- Your parents – their marital status, their jobs, etc.
- Your brothers and sisters – how many you have; whether they are older or younger than you; whether they are married, etc.
- Your wife/husband (if you are married)
- Your children (if you have any)
- Other family members (grandparents, cousins etc.) who live with you

Asking for repetition and expressing non-comprehension

Family
Exercise 11

Work with a partner. In which of the two situations below would you ask the interviewer to repeat him or herself? In which would you express non-comprehension?

a The interviewer uses a term that you don't understand, e.g. he or she asks the question: 'Are de facto marriages common in your country?' and you don't understand the expression 'de facto'.

b The interviewer speaks too quickly or too quietly.

Discuss what you would say to the interviewer in the two situations above and write down the phrases you would use. Discuss your answers as a class.

Exercise 12

Look at the following expressions. Did you have any of these in your answers to Exercise 11?
- I'm sorry, could you say that again?
- I'm sorry, I didn't quite catch that.
- What does 'de facto' mean?
- I don't know what 'de facto' means.
- I'm afraid I don't quite understand what you mean.
- Sorry, could you repeat that?
- Sorry, could you repeat your question?

Divide the above expressions between the two headings below:

Asking the interviewer to repeat	Expressing non-comprehension
....	....
....	....
....	....
....	....

Tapescript 7

Listen to the tape to check your answers.

Exercise 13

Work with a partner. Mark where the stress occurs in each phrase in Exercise 12. Listen to the tape again to check your answers. Listen to the tape again and imitate the intonation and stress used.

Exercise 14

Tapescript 8

Listen to the tape and be ready to respond to each question with a suitable expression – either asking for repetition or expressing non-comprehension.

Exercise 15

Work in pairs. Each pair should choose one or two of the sentences below and check the meaning of the underlined word(s) (you can use your dictionaries). Be ready to explain your word(s) to other students. Get help from your teacher if necessary.

Example sentences
- My brother and sister live with their <u>spouses'</u> families.
- I live with my <u>extended family</u>.
- I belong to a <u>nuclear family</u>.
- My mother is a <u>solo parent</u>.
- I have three <u>step-sisters</u>.
- My parents <u>adopted</u> me.

With your partner, imagine a family situation for each of your sentences and describe the situations to each other, including your sentences in your description. We have given you an example below:

Example sentence: My older brother lives with his <u>de facto</u> wife.

Description: I live at home with my parents. My father is a businessman, and my mother is a housewife. I have an older brother, but he doesn't live with us. He lives with his <u>de facto</u> wife and he's a teacher. And I also have a younger sister. She's studying in the States at the moment. She's really intelligent – she's studying for a PhD in Education.

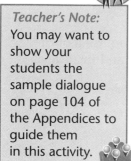

Exercise 16

Teacher's Note:
You may want to show your students the sample dialogue on page 104 of the Appendices to guide them in this activity.

Form two groups. Group A should have a student from each pair (from Exercise 15) and Group B should have the other student from each pair. Mingle with the other students in your group and take it in turns to talk about your imaginary families, including your sentence. Your partner should listen to your description and ask what any new words mean. Explain the meaning of the new vocabulary to your partner.

Exercise 17

Divide the class into three groups. Each group should choose **one** of the topics below. In your group, discuss your answers to the questions for your topic and try to include some new, high-level vocabulary in your answers (you can use a bilingual dictionary if you want). Check with your teacher that you know how to use the new vocabulary and how to pronounce it correctly.

Topic 1 – Language

- How many languages do people in your country use?
- Are different languages used in different regions? Which regions?
- Are different languages used for different media and purposes? Which media and purposes?
- How many writing systems are used in your country?
- Are different writing systems used for different media and purposes? Which media and purposes?

Topic 2 – Ethnic mix

- Do people in your country have different ethnic origins? What are they?

- Which people form the majority of the population?
- What are the differences between people of different origins – physical, customs, clothing, religion, language, food, etc?
- Is there any discrimination; is it positive or negative discrimination?

Topic 3 – Religion

- Is there a variety of religions practised in your country? What are they?
- What is the main religion in your country?
- Is there a state religion? What is it?
- Is religion taught in schools?
- Is religion very important in your country? In what way?
- What religious places/buildings/festivals are there in your country?

Now work in groups of three with one student from each of the three groups. Tell your partners about your topic and include as many new high-level vocabulary items as possible.

Explaining unknown words

Food

Exercise 18

Work in pairs. Discuss what different things you can do to explain a word from your language when you don't know the English equivalent for it.

Exercise 19

Tapescript 9

Listen to the tape where people are describing food that they don't know the English word for. What are they describing?

1 ....

2 ....

3 ....

4 ....

Exercise 20

What information did the people give about the different foods?
Listen to the tape again and put the number **1** next to the
information below in the first description, the number **2** next to the
information given in the second description, etc.
- size
- cultivation
- ingredients
- shape
- colour
- taste
- accompanying food
- uses
- texture

 ## Exercise 21

In your first language, write some names of different foods that you
think are particular to your country or that you can't find in English-
speaking countries:

A fruit or vegetable ....

A dish ....

Some other food (e.g. a grain, meat, etc.) ....

 Now try to describe the foods in English to the rest of the class, but
do NOT say the name of the food. Start with one of the following
expressions:
- I've forgotten the English name for it, but it …
- I can't remember what it's called, but it …
- The name escapes me at the moment, but it …
- I don't know the name for it but it …

As you listen to other students' descriptions, decide if you know the
food they are describing, and if you know what it is called either in
English or another language. If you don't know the food, decide if
you think you would like it.

Describing things

Festivals
Exercise 22

Work in small groups. Discuss which festivals you think the following photos show. Talk about what you can see and which country you think the photo was taken in. Ask your teacher about any vocabulary that you don't know.

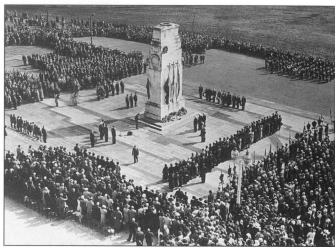

Exercise 23

Work individually. Look at the sentences below. Which festivals are the sentences about?

a People exchange presents

b Fireworks such as rockets, Catherine wheels, bangers and sparklers are set off.

c Soldiers and politicians put wreaths of flowers on war memorials.

d Families meet together for a big meal.

e Bonfires are lit.

f People usually eat turkey.

g People often wear paper hats.

h People gather in parks and other public places at night.

i There are often parades of ex-soldiers.

Exercise 24

Think of a festival that you celebrate in your country. What photos would you take to show a foreigner what happens at that festival?

- If you are in a multicultural class, work on your own to produce drawings of the photos you would take.

- If you are in a monocultural class, work with another student to produce the drawings.

Describing things, asking for repetition and dealing with vocabulary problems

 Festivals
Exercise 25

Mingle with all the other students in the class. Show your pictures to the other students and tell them about the festival you have chosen. You can use the following prompts to give you ideas of what to talk about:
- Food and drink
- Presents
- Events
- People
- Clothes
- Special traditions

As you listen to other students' descriptions, use the expressions from Exercise 12 to ask for repetition and express non-comprehension. If your partners don't understand any of the vocabulary that you use, try to help them with an explanation of the unknown word.

Wedding ceremonies
Exercise 26

Divide the class into teams of three or four students. In your groups, think of vocabulary items (in English) to describe a traditional western wedding. Write them under the headings below.

A traditional western wedding

People   Clothing   Food and drink   Presents   Customs

Find out which team has the longest vocabulary lists.

Exercise 27

Work in two groups. Group A should read the text on page 104 of the Appendices. Group B should read the text on page 111 of the Appendices.

    Work in pairs with one student from Group A and one student from Group B. Tell your partner about the information you have read.

Exercise 28

Have you been to either a traditional or a more modern wedding in your country (perhaps it was your own wedding!)? Work in small groups. Talk about a traditional wedding in your country. You can use the prompts below to help you.
* People
* Clothing
* Food and drink
* Presents
* Customs

Homework
Your home town

Exercise A

Look at the two texts on page 25 which give information about two students' home towns, and underline the parts of the text that give information on the following aspects:

- Economy
- Population
- Location
- Size
- Attractive features

Text 1

I come from Liverpool. It's a large city of around three quarters of a million people and it's in the north west of England, about 250 miles from London. I'm not too sure what the main industries are now … it used to be a major port and it was also important for heavy industries such as ship building and car manufacturing. In recent years that's changed, though, and now the main source of employment is probably the service industries, things like insurance and banking and so on. It's not a very beautiful city any more, either, although I think a hundred years ago it probably was, and it still has some lovely old buildings. To be honest, it's a bit crowded and dirty and noisy because of all the traffic, but the people are really friendly and have a great sense of humour.

Text 2

I live in Christchurch – it's the third largest city in New Zealand with a population of 300 000. It's on the east coast of the South Island and it's not far from the Southern Alps – the main mountain range in the South Island. It's called 'the Garden City' because of all the parks and beautiful gardens. It's quite a busy place and is a main shopping centre for the South Island. There are lots of small manufacturing companies, producing such things as clothing, footwear and electrical goods, and it's rather a cultural centre too, with plenty of cinemas, theatres and art galleries.

Exercise B

Now research information about your own home town. You may need to go to a library. If you have no information on your home town, produce information about the capital city of your country. Make notes under the following headings:

Economy   Population   Location   Size
Attractive features

Be ready to tell another student about your town/capital city next lesson.

Unit 3
Questions and responses

Revision

Work in small groups. Take it in turns to tell each other about your home towns using the information you researched for the homework for Unit 2.

As you listen to other students' descriptions, make notes under the headings below. If you don't understand or can't hear what other students say, ask them to explain things or to repeat what they have said.
- Economy
- Population
- Location
- Size
- Attractive features

After each student has finished speaking, compare your notes.

Asking questions

Exercise 1

Imagine that you are a student at a railway station and want to find out about trains to a city called Hastings. Look at the ideas below and work with a partner to write a conversation between yourself (the student) and an information desk clerk at a railway station.
- Departure time of next train
- Arrival time
- Cost – single/return ticket
- Need for seat reservation
- Platform number
- Buffet car/restaurant car

Put your written dialogue to one side. You will need it again later.

Exercise 2

Work in pairs to discuss your answers to these questions:

a In which section of the interview do you have to ask the interviewer questions?

b What is the interviewer assessing in that section?

Look at the texts on pages 103 and 110 of the Appendices to check your answers to these questions.

 ### Exercise 3

Work in small groups. What different question forms are there in English? We have given you an example:

1 'wh' questions (who, what, how, why, when, where)

2 ....

3 ....

4 ....

5 ....

6 ....

7 ....

Which of the different question forms do you think you should use no more than once in Section 3 of the IELTS interview? Why? Check your answers by looking at the texts on pages 103 and 110 of the Appendices.

 ### Exercise 4

Work in pairs. Look at the prompt card below and discuss the meanings of the prompts with your partner. If you are not sure of any vocabulary, check it in a monolingual dictionary or ask your teacher for help.

PROMPT CARD

Student travelcard

You are a student at college. You want to find out about a student travelcard. Ask the examiner for the following information:

- Cost of travelcard
- Validity period
- Forms of transport covered
- Benefits offered by the travelcard
- Restrictions on use of travelcard
- Where to obtain the travelcard
- Identification required to obtain a travelcard
- Any other documents required to obtain a travelcard

Exercise 5

Tapescript 10

Divide the class into two teams. Listen to the recording of someone asking questions about the 'Student travel' prompt card and write down the questions he asks. (You may want to decide that Student 1 in your team listens for questions 1 and 5, Student 2 in your team listens for questions 2 and 6, Student 3 in your team listens for questions 3 and 7, etc.)

Question 1 (cost)	....
Question 2 (validity)	....
Question 3 (forms of transport)	....
Question 4 (benefits)	....
Question 5 (restrictions)	....
Question 6 (where to obtain)	....
Question 7 (identification)	....
Question 8 (other documents)	....

Compare your answers in your teams.

Exercise 6

Each question in Exercise 5 has a value. If your team can write the question on the board exactly as it was on the tape, your team will be awarded the value for that question, but if you make a mistake, the opposing team will have the chance to correct it and to win the value. Take it in turns to choose a question and write it on the board. The winning team is the one with the most 'money' at the end.

Question 1	$5
Question 2	$10
Question 3	$20
Question 4	$15
Question 5	$5
Question 6	$5
Question 7	$25
Question 8	$10

Exercise 7

Now match each of the eight questions that the student on the tape asked, with the seven different types of question forms in Exercise 3. Check with a partner.

Exercise 8

Look back at the dialogue you wrote for Exercise 1. Work with the same partner that you wrote the dialogue with and decide:

a How many different types of question form did you and your partner use in your dialogue? Give yourselves one mark for every question type that you used. How many marks did you get?

b With your partner, choose one of the three different sets of question types on page 105 of the Appendices. Change the questions in your dialogue to fit the set of question types you have chosen. Make sure that the grammar of your questions is accurate.

Now practise reading your dialogue with your partner.

Exercise 9

With your partner, read out your dialogue from Exercise 8 to the class. As you listen to the other students' dialogues, write down the different types of question forms ('wh' questions, indirect questions, yes/no questions, etc.) in the order that they occur. At the end of each dialogue, check your answers as a class. Did you identify the different forms in the correct order?

Exercise 10

Work in small groups. Say the following sentences out loud and then answer the 'Questions' below them:

Sentences

a Where can I get a **tra**velcard, please?

b Can I use it for trains?

c Can you tell me what the benefits are?

d I'll need to show them some form of identification, won't I?

e Do I pay now or later?

f Does it just cover buses?

g How long is it valid for?

h Are there any restrictions?

i My friends can't use it, can they?

j Is it valid for a year or longer?

k How much does it cost?

l Do you know where I can buy one?

Tapescript 11

Questions

1 Where are the main stresses in the sentences (some sentences have more than one main stress)? We have done the first one for you as an example. Listen to the tape to check your answers.

2 What happens to your intonation on the stressed syllables? Does it go up or down? Listen to the tape to check your answers

3 What general 'rules' can you make about intonation in:
   a 'wh' questions
   b yes/no questions
   c tag questions
   d either/or questions
   e indirect questions

Listen to the tape again and imitate the intonation and stress used.

Exercise 11

Work in pairs. Look at the prompt card below and decide what questions and answers you could make. Write the questions down and check that you have a range of different types of questions. Practise your intonation.

PROMPT CARD

You are a student at a college. You want to know about the student cafeteria on the campus. Ask the examiner questions.

Student cafeteria
- Location
- Type of place – coffee bar, restaurant, cafe, etc.
- Prices
- Range of food and drink available
- Hours of opening
- Interviewer's opinion of the cafeteria

As a class, discuss your ideas for possible questions. Check that they are grammatically accurate.

Work with your partner again. Take it in turns to ask and answer the questions as if you were an interviewee and an interviewer in the IELTS speaking test.

Exercise 12

Mingle with all the other students in the class. Practise asking and answering questions about the student cafeteria again, with as many other students as you can. Take it in turns to ask and answer the questions.
- When you are the **interviewee**, do NOT look at your written questions – ask the questions from memory.
- When you are the **interviewer**, listen to the different types of questions that your partner asks. Check if your partner uses:
  - a good range of different types of questions, and
  - correct intonation patterns.
When your partner has finished, tell them how good their question forms and intonation were.

Responding

Exercise 13

Listen to the tape recording from Exercise 5 again. Decide what is not very good about the interviewee's performance.

Exercise 14

Work individually. Look at the tapescript of the dialogue on page 32 and fill in the gaps with suitable comments from the following list:

Comments
- That's a pity
- Well, it sounds a pretty good deal.
- Oh, it's quite cheap, then.
- I see; so it's $50 per year.
- Just my student card …
- 10%? That's not bad.
- Oh, good. That's handy.
- Well, first of all …
- No, no. Of course not.

Tapescript 12

Interviewee: I wonder if I could ask you some questions about a student travelcard.

Interviewer: Yes, of course. What would you like to know?

Interviewee: .... how much does it cost?

Interviewer: It's $50.

Interviewee: .... But how long is it valid for?

Interviewer: Just a year. You have to renew it each year that you are a student.

Interviewee: .... And does it cover just buses or can I use it for trains and for air travel?

Interviewer: You can use it for intercity coach and rail travel. Not for buses around town or for plane journeys, I'm afraid.

Interviewee: .... Can you tell me about the benefits that having a travelcard would give me?

Interviewer: Sure. You get 10% off both single and return tickets for coach or train travel.

Interviewee: .... Are there any restrictions?

Interviewer: Yes. You can only use it for yourself; you can't lend it to a friend or buy tickets for friends with it.

Interviewee: .... So, where can I get a travelcard?

Interviewer: At the Students' Union Office here on campus.

Interviewee: .... I'll need to show them some form of identification, won't I?

Interviewer:	Yes. You'll need to take your student card with you, to prove you are eligible for a Student Travelcard.
Interviewee:	.... or do I have to take any other documents with me?
Interviewer:	Just a passport size photograph.
Interviewee:	.... Thanks for the information.

Check your ideas by listening to the tape recording. Practise reading the dialogue with a partner.

Exercise 15

Work in small groups. Look at the prompt card below and discuss what questions you could ask the interviewer. Make sure that you have a range of different question types.

PROMPT CARD

The examiner belongs to a film club. You are interested in joining the club yourself. Ask the examiner questions about the following:

Film club

- Cost of membership
- Cost of tickets
- Types of film shown
- Number of screenings per week
- Location where films are screened/shown
- Possibility of bringing friends

Look at the script below. Try to find questions similar to the ones you wrote.

Script

Interviewee:	I hear you belong to a film club.
Interviewer:	Yes, that's right.
Interviewee:	Well, I'm interested in joining myself, but I wondered if you could tell me a bit about the club.

Interviewer: Sure. What do you want to know?

Interviewee: Well, how much does it cost to become a member?

Interviewer: It's $100 a year.

Interviewee: .... So are the tickets quite cheap?

Interviewer: Yes, very cheap – just a dollar each.

Interviewee: .... But what sort of films do they show? I mean, are they well-known ones or old ones or what?

Interviewer: They're mainly European – you know, French, Spanish, British, even Polish. Art films really. Definitely not action films like 'Rambo' or 'Terminator' and so on.

Interviewee: .... And the films are on every evening, seven days a week, are they?

Interviewer: No. Just two evenings a week – Thursday and Friday.

Interviewee: .... So where are they shown?

Interviewer: In the theatre of the town hall.

Interviewee: .... If I become a member can I bring a friend with me, or does my friend have to be a member too?

Interviewer: No. You can bring one friend with you.

Interviewee: .... Do they pay just $1 for their ticket too?

Interviewer: Oh, yes. It's just a dollar for them too.

Interviewee: .... Well, I think it sounds quite interesting. Maybe I'll join.

Exercise 16

Work in pairs. Look at the script above again and decide what you could put in the blank spaces. Practise the dialogue with your partner.

 ## Exercise 17

Mingle with the other students in the class. Talk to as many other students as you can. Take it in turns to be the interviewer and the interviewee talking about the Film Club but do NOT look at the written dialogue in Exercise 15.

- When you are the **interviewee**, look at the prompt card in Exercise 15.
- When you are the **interviewer**, use the answer card below. In addition, when you are the interviewer, listen to the interviewee's question forms and his or her responses to your answers. At the end of the interview, tell the interviewee how well you thought he or she spoke.

ANSWER CARD

> **Film Club**
> - Cost of membership — $100 per year
> - Cost of tickets — $1
> - Types of film shown — European (French, Spanish, British, Polish) Art films
> - Number of screenings per week — Two evenings a week (Thursday and Friday)
> - Location where films are shown — The theatre in the town hall
> - Possibility of bringing friends — One friend only ($1 per ticket)

 ## Exercise 18

Work in groups of three. Look at the prompt card below and discuss the meaning of the prompts and what could be suitable questions. Ensure that you think of a range of different question types ('wh' questions, indirect questions, yes/no questions, etc.), but do NOT write the questions down.

PROMPT CARD

> **Overseas Students' Support Office**
>
> You are an overseas student at a college. Ask the examiner for information about the Overseas Students' Support Office. You can use the following ideas:
>
> - Who the Support Office is for
> - What services are offered
> - Location of the office
> - Hours of opening
> - Fees charged
> - Need for appointments

Take it in turns for one student to be the interviewer, another student to be the interviewee and the third student to listen and make notes about how well the interviewee:

a asked questions
- were they grammatical?
- was the intonation and stress right?
- was there a range of different question types?
b responded to the interviewer's answers.

If there are any problems, practise the interview again.

 Exercise 19

Work in pairs. Look at the prompt cards below and discuss the questions you would ask and the range of question forms you would use. As you discuss your ideas, notice what is different about the questions you would ask for these two new prompt cards compared with the other earlier prompt card questions in this unit.

PROMPT CARD

The examiner has just won a competition for a scholarship to study overseas. Ask him or her questions about it. You can use the following ideas.

The scholarship

- What the competition involved
- Number of people who entered the competition
- The judges of the competition
- How the judges chose the winner
- Location of overseas studies
- Departure date for overseas studies
- His/her feelings about studying overseas

PROMPT CARD

The examiner has recently had a birthday party. Find out information about the party by asking questions about the following:

The birthday party

- Date
- Type of party
- Number of people who attended
- Any gifts received
- His/her feelings about the celebrations
- Plans for future celebrations
- Reasons for future plans

 Compare your ideas with those of another pair of students.

Exercise 20

Work individually. Look at the questions below for 'The scholarship' prompt card. Find the mistakes and correct them.

a Can I ask what did the competition involve?
b Have many people entered the competition?
c Who has judged the competition?
d How the judges chose the winner?
e Where you are going to study overseas?
f Do you going overseas next term or not till next year?
g I imagine you are excited about going overseas, aren't I?

In pairs, discuss why the questions above are incorrect. Check your answers as a class.

Exercise 21

Work in small teams. Write the questions for 'The birthday party' prompt card. Think carefully about the tenses and the question forms that you use. When you are sure your questions are perfect, write each word on a separate piece of paper as in the example below (include capital letters for the first word of each sentence and the question mark at the end of the last word):

Where	did	you	celebrate	your	birthday?

Did	you	get	any		presents?

Now jumble up all the pieces of paper and give them to another team to try and reproduce your original questions.

Exercise 22

Work in pairs with students from different teams in each pair. Take it in turns to be interviewer and interviewee. Use the prompt cards on page 36 to ask and answer questions about 'The scholarship' and 'The birthday party'. Do NOT look at the questions you wrote or the questions in the book. The interviewer should listen to decide how well the interviewee:

a asked questions
- were they grammatically correct?
- was the intonation and stress right?
- was there a range of different question types?

b responded to the interviewer's answers.

If there are any problems, practise the interview again.

Exercise 23

Divide the class into two groups: Group A and Group B. Group A students look at prompt card A below; Group B students look at prompt card B below. In your groups, work together to decide what questions you could ask. Make sure you have a variety of different question types, but do NOT write them down.

PROMPT CARD A

You have heard that there is going to be a student barbecue. Ask the examiner for information.

Student barbecue

- Location of barbecue
- Date and time
- Means of transport to the barbecue
- Cost
- Provision of food and drink
- Who can attend

PROMPT CARD B

The examiner has asked you to buy a raffle ticket. Find out about the raffle by asking questions.

Raffle ticket

- Cost of tickets
- Prizes
- Charity involved
- Date of raffle ticket draw
- How the winners will be notified
- When the winners will be notified

Exercise 24

Group A students should now look at prompt card B and Group B students should look at prompt card A. In your groups, work together to decide what **answers** you could give to any questions you are asked from the prompt card.

Exercise 25

Work in pairs with one student from Group A and one student from Group B. First, Group A students should ask questions about prompt card A and Group B students should answer them. Next, Group B students should ask questions about prompt card B and Group A students should answer them.

Exercise 26

Change partners, but still have one Group A student and one Group B student in each pair. This time, Group A students should ask questions about prompt card B and Group B students should ask questions about prompt card A. When you are the interviewer, listen to the interviewee's question forms and responses to your answers. At the end, tell the interviewee how well you thought he or she spoke.

Homework

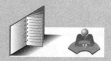

1 Match the following descriptions with the illustrations on page 40:

Descriptions

- It's made of wood.
- It consists of two storeys
- It's got a flat roof.
- It has a verandah.
- It has a balcony.
- It's built of brick.
- It's got ranch sliders.
- The windows have small panes of glass.
- It has large picture windows.
- There's an integral garage.
- The garage is under the house.
- It's built on stilts.
- The roof is thatched
- It has a tile roof.
- It's on the third floor of a modern apartment block.
- It's made of concrete.
- The walls are made of mud and straw.
- It's got a pitched roof.
- The roof is made of sheets of metal.

2 Draw a picture of one of the following things:
- your own family home
- a traditional house in your country
- your dream home.

Make sure you know the vocabulary you need to describe the house, and be ready to give a description of it to other students in the next lesson.

Unit 4
Comparisons

1 As a class, check your answers to the homework.

2 Work in small groups. Show the picture you drew for homework to the other students in your group and describe the house. When you have finished, ask the other students to decide if you have been talking about your own family home, a traditional house in your country or your dream home.

3 Mingle, and ask questions about other students' family homes. Use a range of question forms ('wh' questions, yes/no questions, either/or questions, tag questions, indirect questions, etc.) and try to use suitable intonation patterns. Form groups with other students who have similar homes. Each group should report their findings to the class.

Comparing and contrasting – comparative adjective forms
People

Exercise 1

Work in small groups.

- If you are studying in an English-speaking country, talk about the differences between the people in that country and the people in your own country.
- If you are studying in your own country, talk about the differences between people from two different regions of your country.

Some of the things you could talk about are:

- Physical characteristics (height, build, hair colour, hair style, eye colour, skin colour, facial shape, facial features, etc.)
- Character (outgoing, noisy, friendly, hardworking, funny, happy, etc.)
- Clothing (styles, materials, colours, etc.)
- Language
- Customs
- Religion

Exercise 2

Spot the differences. Work in pairs. Student A in each pair should look at the picture on page 106 of the Appendices; Student B in each pair should look at the picture on page 112 of the Appendices. Do NOT look at each others' pictures. Describe your pictures to each other so that you can find all the eight differences.

Exercise 3

As a class, discuss which of the differences between the pictures are large differences and which are small differences. Use the following structures:

Big differences	Small differences
X is/are much .... er than Y	X is/are slightly .... er than Y
more	more ....
less	less ....
X is/are a good deal .... er than Y	X is/are a little .... er than Y
more	more ....
less	less ....

Exercise 4

Work individually. Decide how you would describe yourself in relation to the average man or woman in your country. Write between 7 and 10 statements about yourself based on the sentence patterns below, including 2 statements that are NOT true.

a I'm
much taller than most people
of about average height
slightly shorter than average

b I've got
hair a good deal longer/darker than average
average-length/colour hair
hair a little shorter/fairer than most people

c I'm   much bigger than average
                    of average build
                    a little more petite than most people

d My nose is   much smaller than most
    My eyes are   normal size
    My ears are   slightly larger than most
    My mouth is

e I speak   a good deal more quietly/quickly than most
                    at about the same volume/speed as most people
                    a little more loudly/slowly than average

f I'm   much more self-confident/extrovert than average
                    not particularly self-confident/extrovert
                    slightly more shy/introvert than most people

Work in small groups. Read out your description of yourself to the other students. Listen to what other students in your groups say about themselves. As you listen, try to identify the two statements that are untrue.

Exercise 5

As a class, write the names of between 6 and 10 well-known people on the board. The people must be known to everyone in the class, either because they are famous, or because everyone in the class has met them.

Transfer the list onto a piece of paper and cut it up into strips with one name on each piece of paper.

Work in small groups. Each group should take one piece of paper and should discuss how they would describe the person whose name is on the paper by comparing him or her to other people. Do NOT let other teams know who your person is.

Play the following guessing game. Ask the other teams to make sentences of comparison about the person on their paper, for example, about the person's:

- height
- hair (length, colour, style)
- build
- facial features
- voice
- manner of speaking

- personality
- special abilities

e.g. *Team A:* Tell us about your person's hair.
Team B: OK. It's darker than average.
Team A: Tell us about your person's nose.
Team B: This person's nose is smaller than Kurt's!
Team A: Tell us about your person's special abilities.
Team B: This person dances better than anyone in this class!
Team A: Is it Michael Jackson?
Team B: Yes.

Comparing and contrasting – various forms

Roles of men and women

Exercise 6

Work individually. Look at the following statements about the roles of men and women. Are they true of the roles of men and women in your country? If not, change the sentences so that they are true of your country.

- Men are expected to be the breadwinners and generally earn considerably more money than women.
- Women do far more housework than men.
- Women have much more freedom than men.
- More men than women own their own house.
- Childcare is mainly done by men.
- Fewer women than men work as nurses.
- There are an equal number of women and men in managerial jobs.
- The majority of politicians are women.
- Very few women work as teachers.
- A greater number of men than women drive cars.
- Women tend to do less physically demanding jobs than men.
- Most women stop work when they get married.
- Women are more likely than men to pray/worship at a church/temple/mosque/shrine.
- Religious jobs (priests, vicars, monks, imams) are more frequently female than male.

Mingle, and read your sentences out to other students (do NOT show your sentences to other students). Try to find a partner who has all, or nearly all, the same sentences as you.

Exercise 7

Divide the class into two groups. Group A should look at Fig 1 below; group B should look at Fig 2 below. In your groups, discuss the differences between males and females in education in New Zealand as shown in your chart.

Fig 2
Source: Education Statistics of New Zealand (1995) Data Management and Analysis Section, Ministry of Education

Fig 1
Source: *The position of women in the education services – 1991 and 1992* , by Helen Slyfield, Ministry of Education, Demographic and Statistical Analysis Unit (1993)

Teaching staff	Females	Males
Primary		
Principals	579	1591
Teachers	13 908	2034
Secondary		
Principals	53	256
Teachers	5922	4259
Polytechnic		
Principals	2	20
Tutors	2166	2070
University		
Professors	15	392
Lecturers/tutors	487	692

Numbers of Graduates for Selected Bachelors degrees completed in 1993 by field of study

Field of study	Male	Female
Engineering	429	79
Computing	325	78
Religion and Theology	37	22
Commerce and business	1911	1226
Architectural, Resource Planning	197	129
Agriculture, Forestry and Fishing	96	70
Mathematics	100	75
Natural and Applied Sciences	429	444
Law	483	521
Sport and Recreation	69	85
Medical and Health	234	375
Humanities	730	1231
Social, Behavioural, Communication Skills	431	911
Art, Music and handcrafts	94	230
Education	163	743

0% 20% 40% 60% 80% 100%

■ Male ☐ Female

Exercise 8

Work in pairs. Each pair should have one student from Group A and one student from Group B. Tell each other about the information in your figure in Exercise 7.

Exercise 9

As a class, tell each other whether you think the situation regarding male and female teachers, and the choice of university subjects for males and females is similar in your country to the situation in New Zealand.

Exercise 10

Fill in the missing letters to make phrases of comparison and contrast.

A and B are:

e_a_t_y   _h_   s_m_   w_t_   r_g_r_   t_   X.

f_i_   s_m_l_r   _s   _e_a_d_   X.

r_t_e_   d_f_e_t   a_   f_r   _s   X   _s   _o_c_r_.

t_t_l_y   _i_f_r_n_   w_t_   r_s_e_t   _o   X.

Countries
Exercise 11

If 'A' in Exercise 10 above was your country and 'B' was the USA, what words could replace 'X'? e.g.

- 'My country and the USA are totally different with regard to **climate**.'
- 'My country and the USA are fairly similar as regards **food**.'

Write other topics below:

climate   food ....

....

Check your ideas in groups and add any new ideas to your list.

Exercise 12

Work in pairs. Use the phrases in Exercise 10 to make statements about the topics you listed. Compare your country with an English-speaking country or another country that you know, e.g.

'My country and New Zealand/Australia/Britain/Canada are fairly similar as far as climate is concerned.'

 Compare your ideas as a class.

Exercise 13

It is often possible to analyse topics like 'climate' or 'food' into different aspects. Look at the following examples:

 Work in pairs to try to analyse ONE of the following topics:

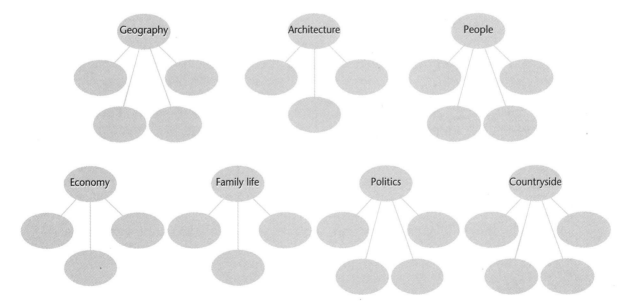

 Mingle with all the other students in the class and tell each other about the different aspects that you thought of for your topic above. Write in the other students' aspects on your paper.

Comparing and contrasting – marker phrases

 ### Exercise 14

Work in pairs. Organise the following expressions into two groups:

similarly	both A and B have/are
in contrast	likewise
as in A, so in Y there is/are	whereas
on the other hand	while

 ### Tapescript 13

Check your answers by listening to the tape.

Mark the main stress in each of the expressions. Check your answers by listening to the tape.

Listen to the tape again and imitate the stress used.

 ### Exercise 15

Work individually. Analyse the following sentences by underlining the topic, the aspect and the comparison/contrast marker.

'My country and New Zealand are totally different with regard to politics. For example, my country has a military government; in contrast, New Zealand is a democracy.'

'My country and Britain are fairly similar as regards food. For example, as in Britain, so in France the staple food is potatoes.'

'My country and Canada are rather different as far as climate is concerned. For example, Canada has four seasons whereas my country has just a wet and a dry season.'

'My country and Australia are exactly the same with respect to family life. For example, both my country and Australia have a large number of solo parent families.'

 Check your answers as a class.

 ### Exercise 16

Work individually. Make six of your own sentences about your country and another country. Include a **topic**, an example of an aspect of the topic and a **comparison/contrast marker**. Use the topic and aspect ideas from Exercise 13.

Work in small groups to compare your sentences. Find out if any students in your group have written exactly the same sentences or if any students have written fairly similar sentences.

Report your findings back to the class.

Education

Exercise 17

Tapescript 14

Listen to the tape of someone talking about the education systems in the UK and in Sweden. Complete the following charts from the information.

Sweden

Age	Institute	Attendance optional or compulsory
5–7	....	....
.....–13	Primary	compulsory
14–16	....	....
16–	....	optional

United Kingdom

Age	Institute	Attendance optional or compulsory
2–5	Nursery	....
....–7	Infants ⎱ Primary	compulsory
8–11	Junior ⎰	
....–16	Secondary	....
....	Secondary/	optional
	....	

Exercise 18

Work individually. Make a chart showing the education system in your country. Use the headings below:

Age	Institute	Attendance optional or compulsory

Divide the class into two groups: Group A and Group B. Look at the instructions for your group below:

Group A

Discuss the similarities and differences between your education system(s) and the Swedish system. Use the language of comparison that you have learnt in this unit.

Group B

Discuss the similarities and differences between your education system(s) and the UK system. Use the language of comparison that you have learnt in this unit.

Form pairs with one student from Group A and one student from Group B. Tell your partner about the similarities and differences between your education system and either that of Sweden or the UK.

Exercise 19

In small groups, discuss your answers to the following questions (answer the questions from memory; do NOT look back at the exercises in the unit):

a What tense(s) have you used so far in this unit?
b What other tense(s) could you use when comparing things?
c What topics have you covered so far in this unit?

Discuss your answers as a class.

Entertainment and hobbies
Exercise 20

Divide into two groups. Group A should look at the instructions on page 106 of the Appendices, Group B should look at the instructions on page 112 of the Appendices.

Society
Exercise 21

Work in three groups. Each group should choose one of the texts below and put the correct vocabulary in the gaps. You may need to use a dictionary. Notice that each text has 9 gaps but 14 vocabulary items.

Crime
Vocabulary

corruption	sharply	hi-jacking	mugging	reached
dropped	driving	manslaughter	robbery	street
slightly	bank	vandalism	theft	

In recent years there has been an overall increase in crime. Certain types of crime have become more common, whilst others have declined. ...., for example, has risen ....– whereas around 2000 people were attacked and robbed in the ....last year, this year the figure ....almost 2800. Similarly, the number of cases of house burglary and of ....from cars has grown. So, too, has the incidence of ...., particularly such things as damage to public phone boxes, to road and street signs, and to street lights. In contrast, some violent crimes, such as murder, ...and sexual attacks, have declined, as has .... fraud and forgery. Drinking and ....has also fallen to a much lower level as a result of the new police campaign.

Politics
Vocabulary

prime	revolution	emperor	democratic	majority
parties	politicians	left	members	government
monarchy	power	president	elected	

Over the last 30 years the country has seen great changes in its political system. A military government was in .... for many years, but this was replaced in 1981 by a .... parliamentary system and , well, in that year a .... - wing socialist government was .... There are now three main ....: that's the socialist People's Party, the right-wing National Party and the central Liberal Democratic Party. And there are around 400 .... of parliament, I think. At the moment, the Liberal Democrats have slightly more MPs than any other party and their leader, the .... minister of the country, is a woman. There are, in fact, four female ministers in the ...., but there are still far more male .... than female.

Marriage and divorce

Vocabulary

adult   get   maintenance   stigma   nuclear   dropped

parent   together   couples   separated   divorce   become

pairs   risen

Up to about 40 years ago, the average marriage age in my country was 20 and couples were married for life because divorce was illegal. Things are totally different now, particularly with regard to marriage age. It's ....considerably and it is now at around 28. Large numbers of people now live ....without getting married. Some ....marry when they decide to have children, but there are also many illegitimate babies born to couples who never ....married, and there is no ....now to having illegitimate children. About one in three marriages break down and end in ...., and there are now slightly more children living in one-...................families than in the traditional .... families. When parents separate, the children usually remain with the mother and the father pays ....money to the mother.

Form groups of three with one student who has worked on each of the above texts. Tell each other which vocabulary items you have put in the gaps. If a student uses vocabulary you don't understand, ask him or her to explain it to you.

 Tapescript 15

Now turn over your book and do not look at it while you listen to the tape recording about crime. When the tape stops, turn your book back over and fill in any gaps that you can remember.

Do the same for the texts on politics and marriage and divorce. Check your answers with the tapescript.

 Exercise 22

How has society changed in your country either in recent years or over a longer period of time? Work in pairs. You can choose to talk about any or all of the following: crime, divorce, role of women, economy, politics, international relations, religion, population, health, transport, etc.

- If you are in a monocultural class, discuss your opinions with another student to find out if you have similar or different opinions about your common country.

- If you are in a multicultural class, discuss your opinions to find out if your different countries have changed in similar ways or in different ways.

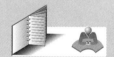 Report your findings back to the class.

Homework

Exercise 23

Decide which of the following statements are true about your country and think of examples or aspects of life to illustrate your opinions.

- It is a slightly more traditional/modern society than most.
- It is a much more/less moral society than most.
- It is misunderstood by other nations or other parts of the world (e.g. Western countries, Eastern countries, non-communist countries, non-Christian countries, etc.).

Be ready to discuss your ideas with other students in the next lesson.

Unit 5
Opinions, ideas and reasons

Revision

Mingle with all the other students in the class and talk to as many other students as you can about the topics you prepared for homework. Try to find other students who have similar opinions to yours.

Expressing opinions, likes/dislikes and preferences

Exercise 1

Work in pairs. Look at the following expressions and organise them under the headings on page 55:

- From my point of view
- I'm not into ...
- I prefer to ...
- It seems to me that ...
- I don't go for ...
- ... appeals to me more.
- As I see it ...
- I'm fond of ...
- I'd rather ...
- In my opinion ...
- I'm not interested in ...
- I'm more attracted to ...
- I'm more interested in ...
- My view is that ...
- The way I see it ...
- ... interests me more.
- I enjoy ...
- I'm keen on ...

Expressing an opinion	Expressing likes/dislikes	Expressing preferences
....	....	....
....	....	....
....	....	....
....	....	....
....	....	....
....	....	....
....	....	....

Exercise 2

In small groups, answer the following questions:

1 In the revision exercise at the beginning of this unit, how many of the opinion expressions do you think you used?

2 Did you mainly, or only, use 'I think' in the revision exercise?

Exercise 3

Work individually. Complete the sentences below by matching the phrases on the left with the words on the right.

From my point of view   books.
I'd rather   reading.
I'm not (particularly) interested in   reading is fun.
                               read.

Now give the four expressions on the right above the correct labels:
- sentence
- verb
- gerund
- noun

Expressing likes/dislikes

Exercise 4

Look back at the likes and dislikes expressions in Exercise 1 and decide whether they can be completed with a sentence, a verb, a gerund or a noun.

Exercise 5

Work in small groups. Complete the following table with suitable gerund phrases to express common activities. We have done the first one for you as an example:

Nouns	Gerund phrases
Heavy metal rock music	- listening to heavy metal rock music - playing heavy metal rock music
Comedy films	....
Science fiction books	....
Busy cities	....
Sports cars	....
Opera	....
Sightseeing	....
Horse riding	....
Competitive sports	....
Team sports	....
Spicy food	....
Art galleries	....
Circuses	....
Zoos	....

Exercise 6

Work in pairs. Mark the main stress on the following likes and dislikes expressions (taken from Exercise 1). We have marked one as an example.
- I en**joy ski**ing.
- I'm keen on skiing.
- I'm fond of skiing.
- I'm not interested in skiing.
- I don't go for skiing.
- I'm not into skiing.

Tapescript 16

Listen to the tape and check your answers. Listen to the tape again and imitate the intonation and stress used.

Work with a partner again and answer these questions:

a Which likes/dislikes expressions have neutral formality and which expressions are informal?

b Which expressions would students talking about pop music probably use?

c Which expressions would a student probably use when talking to a lecturer about a university subject?

d Which expressions would you use in the IELTS interview?

Exercise 7

Work individually. Put the word 'really' into each of the likes/dislikes expressions below.

- I enjoy skiing.
- I'm keen on skiing.
- I'm fond of skiing.
- I'm not interested in skiing.
- I don't go for skiing.
- I'm not into skiing.

Now organise all 12 likes/dislikes expressions (6 with 'really' and 6 without) into 4 groups, from strongest like to strongest dislike:

Group 1 (like a lot)

Group 2

Group 3

Group 4 (not like)

Exercise 8

Work in pairs. Discuss your likes and dislikes with your partner, using the phrases from Exercise 7 to talk about the topics in Exercise 5 (you can use the gerund phrase or the noun). Try to use different likes and dislikes phrases according to how much you like/dislike the activity and how informal you think the topic is. Try to use the correct intonation and stress. Find out how many likes and dislikes you and your partner agree on.

As a class, find out which pair of students had the most similar likes and dislikes.

Exercise 9

Work in small groups. Discuss one or more of the following topics:
- Why you like or dislike living abroad.
- Why you like or dislike your home town.
- Why you like or dislike living with your parents.
- Why you like or dislike travelling.
- Why you like or dislike food from other countries.

Report your group's findings back to the class.

Expressing opinions and giving reasons

Future jobs
Exercise 10

Work in two teams. In your team you have one minute to remember the opinion expressions that were presented in Exercise 1 of this unit. There were six phrases.

Check your answers as a class and find which team remembered the expressions best.

In your teams, answer the following questions:

a Two of the opinion expressions end with the word 'that'. How is 'that' pronounced here?

b How should you complete the opinion expressions (i.e. with a sentence, a verb, a gerund or a noun)?

Exercise 11

Work in pairs. Mark the main stress on the opinion expressions in Exercise 1. We have done one as an example.
- From **my** point of view…
- As I see it …
- In my opinion …
- It seems to me that …
- My view is that …
- The way I see it …

Tapescript 17

Listen to the tape to check your ideas. Listen to the tape again and imitate the intonation and stress used.

Exercise 12

Work with a new partner. Discuss your opinions about the topics below. Try to use a different opinion expression for each topic and use the stress and intonation from Exercise 11. Remember to use the correct grammar to complete your opinion (i.e. an opinion phrase plus a sentence).

Teacher's note:
You may want to show your students the two example dialogues on page 107 of the Appendices.

Smoking	Alcohol	Boxing	American films	Pop music
Motorbikes	Pets			

Exercise 13

What job would you like to do in the future (it may be the near future or the distant future)? Write it at the top of a large piece of paper (e.g. A4 size). Don't let any other students know what you have written. At the bottom of the paper write a number (each student in the class should write a different number). Now give your paper to your teacher who will keep it until you do Exercise 16.

On another piece of paper, list the reasons why you want to do this job and why you think you would be good at it. You do not need to write complete sentences. Put this list away until Exercise 20.

Exercise 14

Tapescript 18

- Listen to the tape recording and write down the reasons why the speaker believes she would make a good hotel receptionist.
- Which reasons that she gives are personal qualities and which are qualifications or skills?
- Listen again and write down the expressions that she uses to give her opinions.

Exercise 15

Work in small groups. Discuss your opinions about which qualities would be desirable for the jobs and professions listed on page 60. Try to use some of the opinion expressions from Exercise 11.

Qualities	Jobs/professions
have a sense of humour	Business manager
have an eye for detail	Accountant
be patient	Interior designer
like working with numbers	Nursery teacher
like working outdoors	Hotel manager
like meeting people	Cabin crew member
like travelling	Doctor
be diplomatic	Ski instructor
be authoritative	
be artistic	
be interested in fabric	
be interested in colour	
be well organised	
be hard working	
be neat and tidy	

Report your opinions back to the class.

Exercise 16

Work in pairs. Your teacher will give you two pieces of paper with a job on each one (the papers from Exercise 13). With your partner, write down the qualities that you think people should have in order to do these jobs well. Write your ideas under each job name. You do not need to write whole sentences. Your paper should look like the following:

> **Hotel receptionist**
> enjoy meeting people
> have a friendly manner
> be patient
> be neat and tidy

When you have finished writing the necessary qualities, fold the job name back so that it can't be seen but the list of qualities can, and put all the pieces of paper in different places round the room.

Exercise 17

Work individually. Write the names of all the students in your class on another piece of paper. Go round the room and decide which list of qualities suits each of the students in your class and write the number that is at the bottom of the qualities list next to the students' name, e.g.

Name	List of qualities
Yun Sook	- paper 5
James	- paper 2
Chien Hsu	- paper 8
Sigrid	- paper 1
Tomoko	- paper 3
Daniel	- paper 7
Toninho	- paper 6
Roberto	- paper 4

Exercise 18

As a class, discuss your opinions as to which student each list of qualities best describes.

Exercise 19

Work in pairs. Look at the word prompts below and try to complete the text of what the girl said on the tape in Exercise 14.

.... like .... hotel receptionist because .... meeting people

.... good receptionist because .... meeting people .... different countries

.... a really friendly manner.

On top .... very patient

Another .... suit me .... neat and tidy.

Finally .... right skills and qualifications .... three languages .... type

.... certificate in hospitality and tourism.

All-in-all, ... right job

.... keen .... chain of hotels.

Tapescript 18

Listen to the tape again and check your answers.

Exercise 20

Work in small groups. Look at the list of reasons that you made for choosing a particular job in Exercise 13. Tell the other students in your group about your reasons. You can talk about any relevant qualities that you have and also about any skills or qualifications that you have. Try to use some of the following language from Exercise 19:

- I'd really like to …
- The way I see it, …
- I'd make a good …
- because …
- On top of that …
- Another reason why I believe it would suit me is …
- Finally, it seems to me that …
- I feel it's the right job for me and …
- I'm really keen on …

As a group, decide if each student gives good reasons for wanting to do their chosen job.

Expressing preferences and giving reasons

Hobbies
Exercise 21

Work in pairs. Try to remember the preference expressions that were presented in Exercise 1 of this unit. There were six phrases. Compare your answers as a class and find which pair remembered the expressions best.

In your pairs, decide:

a How should you complete each preference expression (i.e. with a sentence, a verb, a gerund or a noun)?

b Where is the main stress on the preference expressions?

c Where could you add the word 'much' in each expression to make it stronger?

- I prefer to …
- I'd rather …
- I'm more interested in …
- … appeals to me more.
- I'm more attracted to …
- … interests me more.

Tapescript 19
Listen to the tape to check your answers to questions **b** and **c**. Listen to the tape again and imitate the intonation and stress used.

Exercise 22

Work individually. Look at each of the pairs of activities on page 63 and mark which activity of each two you would prefer. Now decide why you prefer that activity.

Skiing	Reading a book
Watching TV	Going to the cinema
Talking to friends	Going to a disco
Travelling	Staying at home
Listening to music	Going out to a restaurant
Going for a walk	Going to the beach

Exercise 23

Look at the following dialogues in which two people talk about their preferences. Identify any language or function that has been presented or practised in this unit.

Dialogue 1:

A: I'd much rather read a book than go skiing.

B: Yes, I prefer reading too. I'm not really into sports.

A: Me neither. Anyway, the way I see it, skiing is a bit dangerous.

B: Yes and another thing is the cost. It's really expensive.

Dialogue 2:

A: I prefer going to the cinema.

B Really? Why's that?

A: Well, the picture is so much bigger and the sound quality is better.

B: That's true.

A: What about you?

B: Well, actually, watching TV appeals to me much more. For one thing, you can chat to your friends while you're watching. And I enjoy being able to go and get something to eat or drink during the adverts. But the main reason is that it's a lot cheaper!

Practise the dialogues with another student.

Exercise 24

Mingle with all the other students in your class and tell each other your ideas regarding the pairs of activities in Exercise 22. Use

suitable phrases for:
- Expressing likes and dislikes
- Expressing opinions
- Expressing preferences
- Giving reasons for your preferences

Try to find someone else in the class with the same six preferences as you and the same reasons and opinions.

Transport
Exercise 25

Work in small groups to discuss the following:

a what are the most common forms of transport in your home towns for:
- children going to school
- students going to university
- manual workers going to work
- professionals going to work?

b what are the pros and cons of the following forms of transport:

	Advantages	Disadvantages
Bicycles	....	....
Motorbikes	....	....
Cars	....	....
Trains – underground	....	....
Trains – overground	....	....
Buses	....	....

Asking for and giving clarification

Exercise 26

Tapescript 20
Listen to the tape and check if you had the same ideas about bicycles that the interviewee tells the interviewer about.

At times the interviewer did not understand the ideas that the interviewee expressed, even though the language was accurate and quite simple. How did the interviewer ask the interviewee to clarify his ideas? Listen to the tape again and write down the different expressions that the interviewer uses to ask for clarification.

a ....

b ....

c ....

Check your answers by looking at the tapescript.

 Exercise 27

Work in pairs. Discuss whether you think the interviewee clarified his ideas by:

a giving definitions

b giving examples

c repeating what he had already said.

 Listen to the tape again to check your answers.

 Exercise 28

Write down any phrases that you could use for giving examples (you may write down either your own ideas or what you remember from the tape).

1 .... 2..

3 .... 4..

5 .... 6..

 Compare your answers with the tapescript. With a partner, practise the dialogue by reading the tapescript aloud.

Exercise 29

With the same partner, use the conversation outline below to practise:

a asking for clarification

b giving clarification through the use of examples.

Look at the pros and cons you listed in Exercise 25 for ideas about the different forms of transport. Take it in turns to express opinions and to ask for clarification.

Conversation outline

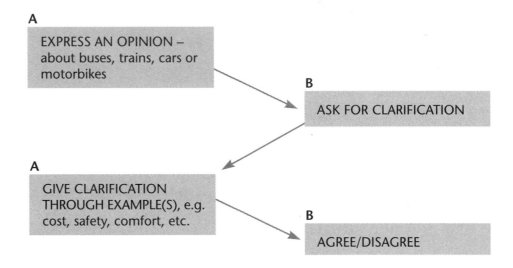

Change partners and practise again, but do NOT look at your books this time.

 Exercise 30

Work in small groups. Discuss your answers to the questions below. If you don't understand something that another students says, ask them to clarify.

a Are traffic congestion and traffic jams a problem in your country?

b Is your government trying to reduce the number of cars in city centres in your country? If so, how?

c What other ways could governments use to try to reduce the number of cars in city centres?

d In your opinion, what is the best way? Why?

Homework
Tourism

Consider what could be the potential benefits and the potential negative effects of tourism on a country and make lists below:

Possible benefits	Possible negative effects
....	....
....	....
....	....
....	....
....	....
....	....

Unit 6
Sequence descriptions

Revision

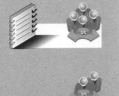

a Work in two groups to compare the lists that you made for homework of the possible benefits and the possible negative effects of tourism.

b Work in pairs. Each pair should have one student from each group. With your partner, discuss whether or not you would like to see an increase in the number of tourists visiting your country and give your reasons. Find out if your partner holds the same views as you. Report your findings back to the class.

Describing a sequence of events

Food
Exercise 1

Work in small groups. Discuss which of the following ingredients you think you would use to make a honey cake and which you would use to make French onion soup (you may need to use a dictionary).

salt	flour	cheese	onion	eggs	garlic	milk
honey	bread	pepper	oil	sultanas	butter	vegetable stock

Which of the following verbs do you think you would read in recipes for the cake and the soup?

slice	fry	grill	boil	simmer	melt	deep-fry
cut	beat	stir	bake	pour	roast	sprinkle
chop	stir-fry	mix	steam			

Tapescript 21

Check your answers as you listen to the tape of people describing how to make the soup and the cake.

Exercise 2

Listen to the tape again and answer the following questions:

a what sequence expressions are used (e.g. 'while', 'then', 'immediately after that')?

b what tense(s) do the speakers use?

Check your ideas by looking at the tapescripts.

Exercise 3

- Divide the class into four groups. Each group should write a description of how to make a simple dish (e.g. baked potatoes, scrambled eggs, noodles, steamed rice). Write between six and eight sentences and write each sentence clearly on a separate line. Try to use some of the sequence expressions from Exercise 2 and remember to use the present simple tense. Do NOT write the name of the dish or the recipe.
- When you have finished writing your description, cut up the paper so that each sentence is on a separate slip of paper. Give the jumbled pieces of paper to another group to put in the correct order. When they have finished, check if the sentences are in the right order and if the other group know what dish the recipe is for.
- Pass your jumbled pieces of paper to another group to put in the correct order.

Exercise 4

Work in pairs:

- If you are in a multicultural class, tell your partner about a recipe for a traditional food from your country. Use suitable sequence expressions and the present simple tense. As you listen to your partner's description, decide if you think you would like the dish or not.
- If you are in a monocultural class, listen to your partner's recipe to check if you think your partner has made any mistakes in his or her description, or if you would make the same food in a different way.

Musical instruments
Exercise 5

Work in small groups.
- List as many musical instruments as you can. You have one minute.
- Compare your lists and find which group has the longest list.

Exercise 6

- Look at the following text and decide what instrument is being described:

I've never played it myself, but I've seen other people play it. It consists of a shaped wooden box with a hole in the middle and a long piece of wood with strings on. The strings are plucked with the fingers of one hand. At the same time, the strings are pressed down at the far end of the long piece of wood with the fingers of the other hand.

- Check your ideas as a class.
- Look at the text again and identify the following:
  - the information about how the instrument is played
  - the tense used in the information about how the instrument is played
  - the information about how the instrument is constructed
  - the sequence expression.

Exercise 7

Work as a class. Describe a traditional musical instrument. In your description, include information about how the instrument is constructed, information about how the instrument is played, a suitable sequence expression and verbs in the present simple passive.
- If you are in a multicultural class, each student should tell the class about his or her national instrument. Students should try to draw the instrument.
- If you are in a monocultural class, work together to produce a description of your national instrument.

Exercise 8

Work in pairs to produce a description of another instrument from the list you wrote for Exercise 5. Do NOT write the name of the instrument in your description. Each pair of students should read out their descriptions to the class for the other students to guess what the instrument is.

Education and work

Exercise 9

Work individually. Look at the notes below and guess the order in which they occurred in someone's life.
- Attended a theatre school
- Gave up working in the theatre
- Worked in a theatre in Norfolk
- Worked at a theatre in Bristol
- Was unemployed
- Left high school
- Went to university
- Worked at a theatre in Liverpool
- Worked in various theatres

Check your ideas in small groups.

Now read the following excerpt of someone talking about their working life and check if you guessed the order correctly.

I left high school in 1968. I had good examination results and got a place at university but I chose not to take it up. Instead, I went to the Old Vic Theatre School. I spent two years there. Then, in 1970, I went to work at the Liverpool Playhouse for a six-month period. Next I got work at the Bristol Repertory Theatre where I spent about three months doing small parts. Then I spent about six months 'resting' – the term actors use when they are unemployed. Then I got a job in a summer theatre in Norfolk. I started with small parts, but then I was given leading roles to play, which was very exciting. Next, I worked in a number of other theatre companies doing a range of acting work. Then, however, I gave up the theatre and went to university after all. But it had been a really exciting five years of my life.

Exercise 10

Without looking back at the text, discuss your answers with a partner:

a   What tenses were used in the text?
b   What aspect of the language in the text could be improved?

Re-read the text to check your answers.

Exercise 11

Work individually. Decide what alternative words and phrases you could use to replace the use of 'then' and 'next' in the above text. Write them down. Compare your ideas in small groups.

Exercise 12

Look at the expressions on page 107 of the Appendices and organise them into groups. Are there any expressions that you did not think of? Can you add any from your own list?

Exercise 13

Look at the expressions again and answer the following questions:
a   What can follow each expression (on the dotted lines) – a sentence, verb, noun, gerund or other grammatical form?
b   Where is the main stress for each expression?

Tapescript 22

Listen to the tape and check your answers to **b**. Listen to the tape again and imitate the stress used.

Exercise 14

Look at the text below. It is the excerpt from Exercise 9 but it has been changed. Put suitable expressions into the gaps from the following list (notice that some have capital letters because they start a sentence):

Then	initially	after
In the end	later	Shortly after
having	first	Subsequently

I left school in 1968. I had good examination results and got a place at university but I chose not to take it up. Instead, I went to the Old Vic Theatre School. I spent two years there. In 1970, ... graduated from drama school, I went to work at the Liverpool Playhouse for a six-month period. .... leaving that job, I got work at the Bristol Repertory Theatre where I spent about three months doing small parts and, ... that, I spent about six months 'resting' – the term actors use when they are unemployed. .... I got a job in a summer theatre in Norfolk. At .... I did small parts, but .... on I was given leading roles to play which was very exciting. ...., I worked in a number of other theatre companies doing a range of acting work. ...., however, I gave up the theatre and went to university after all. But it had been a really exciting five years of my life.

Exercise 15

Work in pairs. Look at the following notes about someone's education from kindergarten through to university and try to write a paragraph using as many of the sequence expressions below as you can.

Year	Event
1973	I went to kindergarten.
1975	I entered primary school.
1981	I took a national examination. I got good marks. I started to study in a high school.
1985	I sat examinations in 11 different subjects. I heard that I had achieved grade A in 8 of the subjects.
1986	I began my studies in a sixth-form college. I specialised in four subjects.
1988	I took the university entrance examination. I was awarded a distinction.
1989	I started studying for an honours degree at university.

Sequence expressions

initially	after that,	after ....ing
in the end	later on	shortly after ....ing
shortly after that,	having ....ed,	subsequently
while	until	after a while,

When you have written your paragraph together, one student should dictate it to the partner to write down so that every student has a copy of the paragraph they wrote with their partner.

Form two groups. Each group should have one student from every pair. Mingle with the other students in your group. Read out your paragraph to as many other students as you can (do NOT show it to them). Try to find another student who has used the same, or nearly the same, sequence expressions as you.

 ### Exercise 16

Work with a partner. Describe your own life since leaving school or, if that was very recently, describe your life since **starting** school. Try to use a range of sequence expressions (you can look at the book for help). Remember to use suitable past tense forms.

When you listen to your partner's talk, note down the expressions he or she uses and check if he or she uses suitable tenses. Give your partner a mark out of ten at the end for his or her use of sequence expressions and tenses!

 ### Exercise 17

Work individually. Choose one of the following topics and make notes (NOT full sentences) about each stage of the process. Try to think of between five and eight stages.

a how you applied to study on the English course that you are currently following (e.g. obtained information about the course, wrote to the institution, sat an examination, paid a deposit, etc.)

b how you applied for a visa or permit to study/live overseas (e.g. obtained an application form, had photographs taken, had a medical examination, sent in the form, etc.).

 ### Exercise 18

Work with a new partner. Tell your partner about the process you made notes about in Exercise 17 above. As you talk, try again to use as many sequence expressions as you can, but this time, don't refer to your book as you speak – try to do it from memory. Remember to use suitable past tense forms too.

Listen to your partner's talk and decide if he or she has missed out any stages. If so, discuss the stages with your partner at the end.

Coping with difficult questions

 ### Exercise 19

What should you do or say if the interviewer in the IELTS examination asks you difficult questions? Work individually to put the suggestions below into rank order from best to worst suggestion.

Suggestions:

a If you don't know the answer to a question, be honest and tell the examiner.

b If you have no ideas or opinions on a subject, be honest and tell the examiner.

c If you don't know the answer to a question, try to think of an answer while saying something else.

d If you don't know the answer to a question, try to think of an answer by considering the question in silence.

e If you have no ideas about a subject, make some tentative guesses and then try to change the subject to something you can talk about.

f If you can't answer a question, tell the examiner that it's a difficult question or that you haven't studied the subject or that you haven't prepared that topic.

 Compare your ideas in pairs and then in groups.

 ### Exercise 20

Tapescript 23

Listen to the two excerpts of students answering an interviewer's questions. Which student do you think responds better to the interviewer's questions?

 ### Exercise 21

Work in pairs. Look at the tapescripts of the two excerpts and match each of the suggestions in Exercise 19 with examples in the texts.
e.g.

Suggestion: b If you have no ideas or opinions on a subject, be honest and tell the examiner.

Examples in the text: 'Um, I'm not sure.'
                                 'I'm sorry. I haven't thought about it.'

Exercise 22

In Text 2 the interviewee uses a variety of expressions to fill in time while he thinks of an answer. Look at the examples below and group similar ones together. Work individually to decide how to describe the groups.

a Oh, that's an interesting question.

b The main differences?

c Oh, er, well ... Yes, ...

d Um, ...

e That's a good question.

f To be honest, I'm not very sure why there are a lot of unemployed young people ...

Compare your answers as a class.

Exercise 23

Work in pairs. Practise the dialogue in Text 2. Take it in turns to be the interviewee.

Exercise 24

Work in the same pairs. Decide how you could respond to the questions below if you were asked them in an IELTS interview. Try to use a range of different strategies from the following list:

Strategies:

a Make some tentative guesses and then try to change the subject to something you can talk about.

b Comment on the question itself.

c Use hesitation devices.

d Repeat (and possibly slightly rephrase) the question.

e Be honest and tell the examiner that you don't know (only use this one if everything else fails).

Questions:

a What was the process by which you obtained a place at high school/university/polytechnic/college?

b How did you learn to drive a car?

c How has your country's economy changed over the years and why?

d How has your country's relations with neighbouring countries changed over the years and why?

e How has your country's attitude to environmental issues changed and why?

f How have attitudes to smoking changed in your country?

g How have attitudes to drinking and driving changed in your country?

Work in new pairs. Take it in turns to ask each other questions from the above list. Listen to your partner's answers and note down which strategies he or she uses for each answer.

Mingle and talk to as many other students as you can. Ask each student you talk to one question from the above list. Listen to your partner's answer and notice:

a what strategies he or she uses

b what sequence expressions he or she uses

c what verb forms he or she uses, e.g. what tenses; active or passive forms.

Tell your partner at the end how well you think he or she answered your question.

Hobbies and skills

Exercise 25

Work in pairs. Look at the text below and decide what functions, strategies or language the interviewer and interviewee use that you have learned in this unit or earlier units in this book.

Interviewer:	You say your hobby is scuba diving.
Interviewee:	Yes. I'm an instructor.
Interviewer:	How did you train to do that?
Interviewee:	I'm sorry, I'm afraid I don't understand what you mean.
Interviewer:	How did you train to be an instructor? How did you learn to teach scuba diving?
Interviewee:	Oh, er. Well, um ... initially, of course, I had to learn to scuba dive myself. I followed a one-week course in New Zealand and subsequently joined a scuba club there and went diving in various places in New Zealand and Australia. After I had made about 50 dives, I decided to become an instructor and took a course specially designed to prepare me for instruction work. Shortly after graduating, I was offered part-time

work at a local scuba-diving club training new divers. And I've worked there ever since.

Interviewer: What does an instructor's course cover?

Interviewee: Well, it covers a number of different things, really, ...er... for example, um, how to maintain equipment, safety procedures, how to deal with accidents and so on.

Interviewer: It's a very dangerous sport, isn't it?

Interviewee: In my opinion, if you're safety conscious it's only a little more dangerous than riding a horse or skiing.

Interviewer: I see. And what sort of equipment do you need to go scuba diving?

Interviewee: Quite a lot – an air tank, of course, and a wet suit. Also things like a BC and a ...

Interviewer: Sorry, what does BC mean?

Interviewee: It stands for buoyancy compensator. It's actually a sort of jacket that you can fill with air so that you float on the surface of the water.

Interviewer: Ah. And is all this equipment very expensive?

Interviewee: I'm afraid I'm not too sure how much things cost these days because I bought all my equipment some time ago. But scuba diving is such fun that it's worth the money – there's so much to do and see underwater. You can explore wrecks and caves, catch fish and lobster and so on, or just look at the plants and animals that live underwater. And underwater photography is very popular too.

Interviewer: Mmm. Yes, I must say it sounds very interesting.

Exercise 26

Look at the following groups of vocabulary and decide what sort of activity each group of words refers to (you may have to use a dictionary):

a ....
colour
black and white
snapshots
portraits
landscapes
zoom lens
wide-angle lens

b ....
singles
doubles
grass court
asphalt court
forehand
backhand
serve

c ....
one hand
both hands
scales
chords
sight reading
playing by ear
white/black keys

d ....
parallel turns
beginner's slope
T-bar
parallel skis
snowplough
chair lift
intermediate run

e ....
dog paddle
breaststroke
floating
diving
freestyle
shallow
deep

f ....
helping my mother
lessons at school
cooking for myself
cooking for friends/family
simple foods
snacks
full meals

Work in small groups. Each group should consist of students who have learnt to do one of the above activities in real life. In your groups, discuss how you learnt the activity, which skills you learnt first, where you learnt, etc.

Teacher's Note: If these activities are not suitable, think of others that students in your class have learnt and decide on some useful vocabulary to describe the different skills involved in each activity.

Mingle and talk to as many other students as you can. Ask each student you talk to which activity they have learnt. Then ask them questions about how they learnt it – the stages, who helped them, where they learnt, etc. Use a range of questions ('wh' questions, yes/no questions, either/or questions, etc.).

Homework

Divide the class into two groups. Group A should look at the information on page 107 of the Appendices and Group B should look at the information on page 113 of the Appendices.

Unit 7
Plans and ambitions

Revision

1   Work in pairs. Every pair should have one student from each group that you formed for the homework exercise at the end of Unit 6. Ask your partner the questions you prepared for homework.

2   Discuss with your partner your answers to these questions:
   a   what is this revision exercise intended to revise?
   b   did you use the language that this revision exercise is encouraging you to use? If not, do the activity again with a new partner.

Expressing plans, hopes and ambitions; giving reasons

Exercise 1

- Work individually. Think about your plans for the future (next month, next year, in five years, in ten years). Consider the following points:
   a   future studies or training courses you want to do
   b   your future career or jobs you want to do
   c   your family and what you hope they will do
   d   places where you want to live.
   Use a dictionary to check any vocabulary you will need, so that you can tell other students about your plans.

- Work in small groups. Tell each other about your plans for the future. Listen to what other students say and decide if any students have similar plans to you or if any students have particularly surprising or exciting plans.

Exercise 2

In your vocabulary books, write down any new vocabulary that you or other students in your group used. Make sure you know the word stress for the new vocabulary and the word class (noun, verb, adjective, etc.).

Exercise 3

As a class, compare your groups' plans for the future and tell each other about any new vocabulary that students in your group used.

Exercise 4

Divide the class into two groups: Group A and Group B. Look at the instructions for your group below:

- Group A. Work in pairs. Organise the following vocabulary into pairs of words with similar meanings:

a job	a field of study	certain	to plan on
an opportunity	to intend to	a firm	an aim
a position	a subject	a goal	initial
a need	a company	a demand	first
a chance	definite		

Now mark the word stress on the words with more than one syllable.

What part of speech (e.g. noun, verb, adjective, gerund) can follow the expressions 'to plan on' and 'to intend to' in the above list?

Check your answers with all the students in Group A, then check your answers in a dictionary.

- Group B. Work in pairs. Match the vocabulary on the left with a word on the right that means almost the same:

initially (adv)	job
ultimately (adv)	expect
ideally (adv)	think
rapidly	do
believe (v)	would like
complete (v)	at first
anticipate (v)	best of all
hope (v)	in the end
post (m)	finish
carry out (v)	fast

In general, which of the above columns of vocabulary is more suitable for a formal conversation about future plans – the left-hand column or the right-hand column? Now mark the word stress on the vocabulary in the left-hand column above.

Which of the following is grammatically correct for the verbs 'hope', 'expect', 'think', 'would like' and 'anticipate' in the above list (you may to need to use a monolingual dictionary)?

1 a   I hope I'll get a job as a journalist.
  b   I hope to get a job as a journalist.

2 a   I expect I'll enjoy my university course.
  b   I expect to enjoy my university course.

3 a   I think I'll find living abroad very interesting.
  b   I think to find living abroad very interesting.

4 a   I would like having a holiday soon.
  b   I would like to have a holiday soon.

5 a   I anticipate starting work soon
  b   I anticipate to start work soon.

Check your answers with all the students in Group B, then check your answers in a dictionary.

Exercise 5

Work in pairs. Every pair should have a student from Group A and a student from Group B. Tell each other about your findings from Exercise 4. Write the information down in your vocabulary book, including the word stress and any information about the grammar.

Exercise 6

Tapescript 24

Listen to the two taped dialogues between a student and an IELTS interviewer. What are the good and bad points of the student's answers in Dialogue 1? What are the good and bad points of the student's answers in Dialogue 2? Discuss your ideas in groups.

Exercise 7

Work individually. Improve what the student says in Dialogue 2, by adding the following comments to what she said. Match the comments with the functions (given in capital letters) on the next page. When you have finished, compare your answers with another student by reading out what you have written (do NOT show your partner your book).

Comments:

a Initially, I anticipate working as a hotel receptionist, but I hope to work my way up into hotel management.

b because, in my opinion, living and working in another culture is very stimulating, and also because I'd like to use my English language skills.

c Another reason is that I enjoy meeting people and making contact with people from overseas, so I feel that I'm well suited to working in the field of hospitality and tourism.

d Ideally, I'd like to work in a hotel in an English-speaking country.

e such as the Hilton Group.

f The tourist industry in my country is growing rapidly and there is a real demand for people with such a qualification.

Interviewer: According to your CV, you're going to study hospitality and tourism. Why have you chosen that particular subject?

Student: **GIVES REASON (OPINION): I believe a qualification in hospitality and tourism will provide me with the necessary skills for a job in the hotel industry.**

PROVIDES SUPPORT FOR OPINION ....

....

GIVES A SECOND REASON ....

....

....

Interviewer: I see. And what will you do after you complete your hospitality and tourism course?

Student: **OUTLINES FUTURE WORK PLANS: I intend to return home and I'll probably apply for a position with an international chain of hotels.**

GIVES AN EXAMPLE ....

GIVES FURTHER DETAILS OF FUTURE WORK PLANS

....

Interviewer:	And what is your ambition?
Student:	**STATES AMBITION: Ultimately, I plan on becoming a hotel manager.**
	GIVES DETAILS OF AMBITION.................................
	....
	PROVIDES REASONS ....
	....

 ## Exercise 8

Work in pairs. Try to improve the student's responses in Dialogue 1 by putting the following comments into the spaces below in the correct order:

Comments

a I have no definite plans at the moment, but I expect I'll start by applying for a junior post in the accounts department of a large organisation.

b It's a subject that I've always enjoyed, and as a high school student I did well in it.

c In addition to providing me with initial work experience, it would give me the opportunity to see the range of work that a large accounts department carries out.

d I believe that I'd prefer to be my own boss rather than work for someone else.

e My ultimate ambition is to have my own successful accountancy firm. It is, of course, a long-term goal but

f an international company, for instance.

g Also, I believe that there are good job opportunities for people with accountancy qualifications.

Interviewer:	On your CV, you state that you're applying for a course in accountancy. Why have you chosen that particular field of study?
Student:	....
	....

....

....

Interviewer: I see. And what exactly will you do after you complete your accountancy course?

Student: ....

....

....

....

Interviewer: And what is your ambition?

Student: ....

....

....

....

Now match the following functions with the comments **a–g** above:

- GIVES AN EXAMPLE
- GIVES A REASON FOR AMBITION
- STATES AMBITION
- OUTLINES POSSIBLE FUTURE WORK PLAN
- GIVES REASONS FOR WORK PLAN
- GIVES A SECOND REASON
- GIVES A REASON FOR SUBJECT CHOICE

Exercise 9

Work individually. Look at the three interviewer's questions on page 86 and the interviewee's possible response functions (in capital letters). Think about the information that you would provide about yourself. Make notes if you want to, but do NOT write whole sentences.

Teacher's Note:
There are alternative questions on page 108 of the Appendices for use with students applying for New Zealand residence.

1   On your Personal Details form, you state that you're applying for a course in ....
    Why have you chosen that particular field of study?

    GIVE A REASON/OPINION ....

    PROVIDE SUPPORT FOR OPINION ....

    GIVE ANOTHER REASON ....

    GIVE EXAMPLE(S) ....

2   And what exactly are you planning to do after you complete your course?

    OUTLINE FUTURE WORK PLAN ....

    GIVE DETAILS OF WORK PLAN ....

    GIVE REASONS FOR WORK PLAN ....

3   And what is your ambition?

    STATE (CAREER) AMBITION ....

    GIVE DETAILS OF AMBITION ....

    PROVIDE REASONS FOR AMBITION ....

Exercise 10

Divide the class into two groups: Group A and Group B. Look at the
instructions below for your group.
• Group A. Work together to find and underline the following
  expressions in the dialogues in Exercises 7 and 8 (not all of them
  appear in the dialogues). Check that everyone in your group
  understands what all the expressions mean.
  - initially
  - I plan on + gerund
  - I anticipate + gerund
  - for instance

- qualification
- a position
- a long-term goal
- job opportunities
- an organisation
- I believe
- another reason is

Now work individually to try and decide how you could use these phrases in your answers to the three interviewer's questions above in Exercise 9.

- Group B. Work together to find and underline the following expressions in the dialogues in Exercises 7 and 8 (not all of them appear in the dialogues). Check that everyone in your group understands what all the expressions mean.
  - ultimately
  - I intend to + verb
  - I expect to + verb/I expect I'll + verb
  - such as
  - field of study
  - a post
  - my ultimate ambition
  - initial work experience
  - no definite plans
  - a firm
  - ideally
  - I'm well suited to

Now work individually to try and decide how you could use these phrases in your answers to the three interviewer's questions above in Exercise 9.

Exercise 11

Work in pairs with one student from Group A and one student from Group B. Take it in turns to be the interviewer and the interviewee.

The interviewer should ask the questions from Exercise 9. The interviewee should include as many of the phrases as they can from Exercise 10 in their answers to the interviewer's questions.

When you are the interviewer, listen to the responses your partner gives and write down the words or phrases that you think your partner has tried to include. (The interviewee can look at Exercises 9 and 10 as they answer the questions, but the interviewer can only look at Exercise 9.)

Exercise 12

Now find another partner and take it in turns to interview each other, using the same three questions from Exercise 9. This time, however, the interviewee must NOT look at Exercises 9 or 10 but must speak from memory.

Exercise 13

Work in small groups. Organise the following phrases into three groups:
- could
- option
- or
- alternative
- alternatively
- might
- on the other hand
- possibility
- choice
- may
- as an alternative
- potential

Now mark the stress on each expression that has more than one syllable.

Tapescript 25

Listen to the tape to check your answers. Listen to the tape again and imitate the stress in the Group 2 and Group 3 expressions.

Exercise 14

In dialogue 1 of Exercise 6 the student didn't have any definite plans for the future because he hadn't thought seriously about it. But perhaps you don't have any definite plans because you think there are different paths that you could take in your future life.

Work in pairs. Look at the flow chart on page 89. If this was about your possible future, what would you say to an IELTS interviewer in answer to the question 'What are planning on doing after your university course?' Write a dialogue of about eight lines with your partner based on the information in the flow chart.

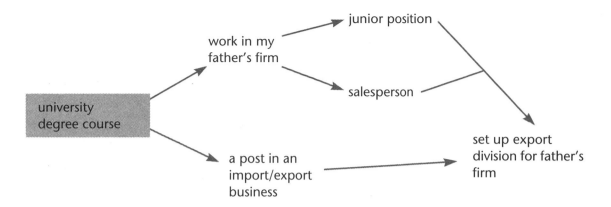

Exchange your dialogue with another pair of students. Read what the other students have written and notice if they have used any expressions from Exercise 4 and Exercise 10. Give them a mark out of 10 for their use of expressions from Exercises 4 and 10.

Now check if they have used any of the expressions from Exercise 13 above. If necessary, change their dialogue so that it includes at least five expressions from Exercise 13. When you have finished, return the dialogue to the original writers.

When you receive your own dialogue back, check what mark the other students gave you and what they have changed.

Exercise 15

Tapescript 26

Listen to the tape and compare your dialogue with what the student says about his future plans. What similarities and what differences were there?

Exercise 16

Work as a class. Look at the tapescript and discuss what expressions you could use to replace the ones that have been underlined.

Work individually to fill each gap in the text with one of the different expressions that you have just discussed:

.... my university course, I .... home and look for

work. At the moment I'm not entirely sure what I'll do; I .... apply

for a .... in an import-export business, ideally working in some way

that I can use my English language skills. .... I ....

take up a job in my father's .... – he has a business manufacturing

electrical components. One .... would be to start in a junior

.... and learn about the business by working my way up through

the different departments in the I

.... begin work as a sales person in order to gain experience in

marketing because my ultimate .... is to set up an export division for

my father's firm and sell the company's products overseas.

Mingle as a class. Read your paragraph out to other students (do NOT show it to them) in order to find another student who has written the same, or nearly the same, expressions as you in the gaps.

Exercise 17

- Work individually. Draw a flow chart to show different options that you could take in your future life and write short notes in the boxes.

- Work in pairs. Tell your partner about your future options using the language from Exercise 13 as well as some expressions from Exercises 4 and 10.

As you listen to your partner, try to draw a flow chart for their future; make notes in the boxes. When you have finished, compare your flow charts to see if you understood what your partner said about his or her future. If there were mistakes or differences, decide if it was your partner's fault or your own fault!

Expressing desire and interest

Exercise 18

Tapescript 27
Listen to the phrases on the tape and write them under the correct headings on page 91:

Expressing desire to do something	Expressing interest in something
....	....
....	....
....	....
....	....
....	....
....	....

- Work in pairs to mark the main stress on each expression. Listen to the tape to check your answers. Listen to the tape again and copy the intonation and stress used.
- Work in pairs to decide what can follow the 'desire' expressions and what can be used in the 'interest' expressions (e.g. noun, verb, gerund, sentence).

Exercise 19

In small groups, discuss what personal ambitions (i.e. ambitions that are NOT related to work, a job or a career) you have.

Tapescript 28

Now listen to the tape recording of a student talking about his personal ambitions. Make notes of what he says.

In your groups, discuss whether anyone has any ambition similar to the ambitions of the student on the tape. Report your findings to the class.

Exercise 20

In pairs, decide if you think the student on the tape used any of these three functions below in answer to the interviewer's question:

- OUTLINES AN AMBITION
- GIVES DETAILS OF AN AMBITION
- GIVES REASONS FOR AN AMBITION

Check your ideas by listening to the tape again.

Now underline the three functions on the tapescript on page 92:

| Interviewer: | Do you have any particular personal ambitions? |
| Student: | Personal ambitions? Well, yes, I suppose I do, actually. I'd really like to visit Lhasa – you know, the capital of Tibet. It's about 3500 metres high, up in the Himalayan mountains. I'm fascinated by Tibet and by the Tibetan Buddhist religion and I'd love to see the monasteries in Lhasa, and the Tibetan pilgrims who go there. And another ambition of mine is to speak Samoan fluently. I'm really interested in learning languages – I can speak three quite well – and there's something particularly beautiful about the sound of the Samoan language – I find the Samoan accent really attractive. So I'd love to be able to speak it well, you know, and with a good accent. |

Exercise 21

Work in pairs. Take it in turns to ask and answer the question 'Do you have any particular personal ambitions?' Remember to include details, information on alternatives, and reasons for your personal ambitions.

Exercise 22

Work as a class. Discuss what you remember about Section 3 of the IELTS interview and produce of list of dos and don'ts. Check your answers by looking at the texts on pages 103 and 110 of the Appendices.

Exercise 23

- Work in two groups. Group A should look at the instructions on page 109 of the Appendices. Group B should look at the instructions on page 113.
- Work in pairs. Each pair should have one student from Group A and one student from Group B. Take it in turns to be interviewee and interviewer. Group A students should ask questions about the prompt card on page 113, and Group B students should ask questions about the prompt card on page 109.

Homework

Think about your answers to the following questions:
- What are you going to do to celebrate the end of your IELTS course/studies?
- What are you going to do after the IELTS examination itself?
- When are you next going to return to your home country?
Be ready to tell other students about your ideas or plans in the next lesson.

Unit 8
Future uncertainties

Revision

a In small groups, discuss your answers to the three questions from the homework exercise in Unit 7, i.e.:
  - What are you going to do to celebrate the end of your IELTS course/studies?
  - What are you going to do after the IELTS examination itself?
  - When are you next going to return to your home country?

b In your groups, decide:
  - What was the aim of revision exercise **a**?
  - Did you use the language and functions that revision exercise **a** was aimed at reviewing? If not, do the activity again in new groups

Hypothesising

 Exercise 1

Work individually. Complete these sentences:

If I .... 4.5 in the IELTS examination I ....

If I .... 5.5 in the IELTS examination I ....

If I .... 6.5 in the IELTS examination I ....

If I .... 7.5 in the IELTS examination I ....

 Work in small groups. Tell each other your sentences to see if any students had the same ideas.

 Exercise 2

Work in pairs. Look at the comments on page 94, made by two different students, and decide which of the eight sentences are grammatically correct.

Student A	
a	If I got 4.5 in the IELTS examination, I'd think there was a mistake.
b	If I got 5.5 in the IELTS examination, I'd be really upset.
c	If I get 6.5 in the IELTS examination, I'll be really pleased.
d	If I got 7.5 in the IELTS examination, I'd be amazed.

Student B	
a	If I get 4.5 in the IELTS examination, I'll be really miserable.
b	If I get 5.5 in the IELTS examination, I'll be happy.
c	If I got 6.5 in the IELTS examination, I'd be ecstatic.
d	If I got 7.5 in the IELTS examination, I'd know there had been a mistake.

 Discuss your answers as a class.

 Exercise 3

Work in pairs to answer the following questions:

a What is the difference in meaning between Student A's and Student B's sentence **a.**

b What is the structure in Student A's sentence **a?**

If + ..., I + ...

c What is the structure in Student B's sentence **a?**

If + ..., I + ...

Compare sentences **b**, **c** and **d** for Student A and Student B.

 Exercise 4

• Work individually. Look back at the sentences you wrote in Exercise 1 and decide if they are grammatically correct and if their meaning is what you intended. If not, change them.

 • Compare your sentences with another student's. Explain why you used the first conditional or the second conditional in each sentence.

 Exercise 5

Look at the text on page 95 in which a student is joking about the

IELTS results. Is the student talking about things that he thinks are real possibilities or unreal hypotheses?

Student A:	If I get the grade I need, I'll buy all my classmates a meal at an expensive restaurant. If I buy them all a meal, I'll have no money left. If I have no money left, I won't be able to telephone my family and tell them the good news. If I don't telephone them, they'll get really upset. If they get upset, they'll .....

 Work together as a class. Try to make up a similar sequence of ideas and write it on the board. Start with, 'If I get the grade I need, I'll......'

 ## Exercise 6

Look at the text below. Another student is joking about the IELTS results. Is the student talking about real possibilities or unreal hypotheses?

Student B:	If I got a low grade, I'd burst into tears. If I burst into tears, everyone would stare at me. If everyone stared at me, I'd be really embarrassed. If I was embarrassed, my face would turn red. If my face turned red, people might start to laugh. If they started to laugh, ...

 Work as a class to make up a similar sequence, but this time, take it in turns to say one sentence. Each sentence must start with the idea from the previous student's sentence. Begin with 'If I got a low grade, I'd...'

 ## Exercise 7

Work in pairs. Take it in turns to ask and answer the following question as if you were in an IELTS interview:

Question: If you are unable to get a place at university/polytechnic/college, what will you do?

When you are the interviewee, include the following in your answers:
- conditional structures
- modals such as 'may', 'might' and 'could' (from Unit 7)
- alternative possibilities of what you might do (from Unit 7)

Teacher's Note:
An alternative question for students applying for New Zealand residence can be found on page 109 of the Appendices.

When you are the interviewer, listen to your partner and note how many times he or she uses conditional structures, modals and phrases expressing alternative possibilities. When your partner has finished talking, tell him or her how well you thought he or she spoke.

Expressing uncertainty, supposition and possibility

Exercise 8

Work in teams. See which team can complete the following expressions first (only vowels have been removed):

Uncertainty

_'m n_t t__ s_r_   wh_t /wh_/wh_r_/wh_n/h_w/why ...

_'m n_t _nt_r_ly s_r_

_'m n_t _lt_g_th_r c_rt__n

_t's d_ff_c_lt t_ s_y   wh_t/wh_/wh_r_/wh_n/h_w/why ...

_t's d_ff_c_lt t_ kn_w   wh_t/wh_/wh_r_/wh_n/h_w/why ...

_t r_m__ns t_ b_ s__n   wh_t/wh_r_/wh_n/h_w/why ...

Supposition

I _m_g_n_ ....

I g__ss ....

I s_sp_ct ....

I s_pp_s_ ....

Possibility

I m_y ....

I c__ld ....

I m_ght ....

P_rh_ps ....

M_yb_ ....

_t's p_ss_bl_ th_t ....

Compare your answers as a class.

Exercise 9

Work in pairs. Mark the stress on the 'uncertainty' expressions above.

Tapescript 29

Listen to the tape to check your answers.

Mark the stress on the 'supposition' and 'possibility' expressions. Listen to the tape to check your answers.

Listen to the tape again and imitate the intonation and stress used.

Exercise 10

In groups, discuss your answers to the following questions:

a What problems do you think you may have in your future studies/work/everyday life in a foreign country?

b Why do you think you may have those problems?

c What could you do to try and cope with those problems?

Exercise 11

Tapescript 30

Listen to the tape recording of a student answering three similar questions in an IELTS interview. Make notes of the answers.

In groups, compare your notes and discuss your answers to the following questions:

a Does anyone in your group expect to have the same problem as the student on the tape expects to have?

b Do you think the student has good ideas about how to deal with the problem? Report your ideas to the class.

Exercise 12

Listen to the tape recording again and tick the phrases from Exercise 8 that you hear the student use.

Exercise 13

Tick two phrases from each of the three headings in Exercise 8 (a total of six phrases). Mingle and tell all the other students in the class the phrases you have ticked (do NOT show your book to them). Try and find other students who have ticked four or more of the same phrases as you.

Exercise 14

Work individually. Fill in the gaps in the tapescript below.

Interviewer: What problems do you anticipate encountering in your future studies at university?

Interviewee: Well, I .... I'll have a number of problems, both academically and socially, really. But I suppose the biggest hurdle could be getting to know people. I .... fairly confident .... my ability to cope .... my studies and the academic demands of the course, but I'm not altogether certain if, well, I'll find it easy to make friends .... other students. I imagine I'll .... to know the other overseas students quite quickly .... the International Students' Club, but, well, it remains to be seen if I'll get to know local students – you know, native English speakers – quite so easily. Perhaps I'm worrying unnecessarily, but I think I may .... it difficult to talk to them and well, you know, become friends .... them.

Interviewer: Why do you think it is so difficult for overseas students to make friends with native speakers?

Interviewee: What makes it so difficult? Well, I suspect the primary .... is the language barrier. My formal English is .... a high standard and that will help me with my academic work, but it seems .... me that in order to socialise with other

students I really need informal, colloquial English. And
.... factor is accent; I'm not sure that I'll
understand all the different English accents of the
students. But, ... my opinion, in addition
.... language problems, there's the cultural
gap. I .... that cultural differences may be a
.... reason why it's so difficult for overseas
and native speaker students to, well, really get to
know .... other.

Interviewer: How do you think you could try to actually overcome
the difficulty of making friends with native speaker
students?

Interviewee: That's a good .... I'm not entirely sure, but,
well, I guess the best .... is to try and start
talking about course work ...., maybe, the
end of a lecture or a tutorial; and then when I've
broken the ice .... that way, maybe I could
suggest going .... a cup of tea or coffee.
And .... coffee we might chat about other
things – you know, I could start .... asking
them questions about where they're from and so on. I
know I can manage that sort of social chat, but it's
difficult to know how to continue sometimes, really. I
suppose another .... would be to join a club
– like a tennis club or a photography club – because
that immediately gives you something to talk

...................., you know, to the other people

.... the club. It gives you an interest

.... common that you can start from.

  Compare your ideas in small groups. Listen to the tape again to check your answers.

 ## Exercise 15

Work in pairs. Take it in turns to be the interviewer and ask the questions below. When you are the interviewee, try to use all six of the phrases that you ticked from Exercise 8. When you are the interviewer, write down the six phrases that your partner uses from Exercise 8. At the end, check what you have written with your partner.

Teacher's Note:
There is an alternative Question **a** for students applying for New Zealand residence on page 109 of the Appendices.

a What problem(s) do you anticipate encountering in your future studies?
b What are the reasons for such a problem/problems?
c How do you think you could try and cope with such a problem/problems?

Exercise 16

Find a new partner. Take it in turns to be the interviewer and the interviewee. The interviewer should ask the three questions below:

Teacher's Note:
There is an alternative Question **a** for students applying for New Zealand residence on page 109 of the Appendices.

a What will you do if you are unable to get a place at university/polytechnic/college?
b What problems do you think you may have in your future studies/job/everyday life in a foreign country?
c What could you do to try and cope with those problems?

 ## Exercise 17

Work in small groups. From memory, produce a list of all the functions and skills that the different units of this book have examined. Do NOT look in the book.
e.g. Functions/skills – expressing opinions; asking for repetition; ...

 Compare your answers as a class. Check your answers in the Map of the Book on page vi.

Exercise 18

Work in the same groups again. Divide the functions/skills between all the groups. From memory write two examples of the language for each of your group's functions/skills, e.g.

Functions/skills	Examples
Expressing opinions	In my opinion, ... From my point of view, ...

If you had problems, look back at the units for your functions and check what language expressions were taught.

Exercise 19

Form new groups. Each new group should have one student from the original groups you worked in for Exercises 17 and 18. Tell the other students in your new groups about the language expressions for your functions/skills.

Exercise 20

Divide the class into two groups. Group A should look at the instructions on page 109 of the Appendices; Group B should look at the instructions on page 114.

Exercise 21

Teacher's Note: An alternative set of questions for students applying for New Zealand residence can be found on page 110 of the Appendices.

Work in pairs. Each pair should have one student from Group A and one student from Group B. In your pairs, discuss your answers to the questions below. As you listen to your partner's answers, try to guess which functions he or she is trying to incorporate in his or her answers.

a What are your chances of getting the score you want in the IELTS examination?

b What are the components of your future course of study?

c How many weeks holiday will you have per year?

d What will you do during your holidays?

e How will you be assessed on your future course of study (e.g. by examination or by continual assessment – essay, seminar presentation, etc.)?

f   What are the fees for your future course of study? Would they be more expensive in your own country?

g   Where are you going to live?

h   Why have you chosen to study in a foreign country?

Revision

Exercise 23

Work in pairs. Use the two prompt cards below to practise asking questions and responding to information as in Section 3 of the IELTS speaking test:

PROMPT CARD

The examiner has got a new camera. Ask questions about the camera.	**The new camera** • when purchased • model • price • special features • where purchased • reason for purchase

PROMPT CARD

The examiner organises evening classes at a local college. You would like to join a class to learn how to touch type. Ask the examiner for information about classes.	**Evening classes** • touch typing classes • date and time • length of course • cost • level of class • equipment used

Exercise 24

Turn to page 114 in the Appendices and play the revision board game.

Appendices

Unit 1
Exercise 4

Group A
The IELTS interview

General information

The IELTS interview is conducted on a one-to-one basis; that is, with one examiner (the interviewer) and one student (the interviewee).

The interview usually lasts between 11 and 15 minutes and consists of five phases, or sections, although you may not always be aware of where one phase ends and another begins.

The five phases

In the first phase, you will exchange greetings with the interviewer and answer some personal information questions – questions about yourself and your background.

Then, in the second phase, the examiner will ask you to talk about some aspect of your own background or experience in more detail.

Phase 3 of the interview is a little different from the other phases in that you should ask the examiner questions, instead of the examiner asking you. You will be given a 'prompt card' to guide you as to what questions to ask. The examiner is interested in the range of different question types that you ask – for example, 'wh' questions, yes/no questions, indirect questions, either/or questions, tag questions and so on. It's also important to respond naturally to the information that the examiner gives in his or her answers to your questions.

In phase 4, you will be asked about your plans for future study or work; the examiner may ask you to speculate on any future problems you might have studying or working in a foreign culture. You may also be asked about what the future holds for your country and what your ambitions are in life. The final phase is when the examiner brings the interview to a close and you both say goodbye.

Advice

It is very important that you answer the examiner's questions fully – do not simply answer 'yes' or 'no' to questions. Remember that the examiner cannot judge your level of English if you say very little.

At the same time, do not prepare and memorise 'set answers' to questions you expect to be asked. If the examiner suspects that you are reciting something you have learnt, they will change the subject to something they are sure you will not have prepared. This new topic could be a lot more difficult!

In general, candidates find sections 1 and 5 of the interview quite easy. There is a great range of subjects that you may be asked to talk about in section 2, making it difficult to predict what you will have to speak on, but the subjects are usually things that you are very familiar with and, therefore, you should not find this section too difficult. For most candidates, the more demanding sections are Section 3, when you have to ask a range of questions, and Section 4, when the examiner will ask you to speculate about the future and to give reasons for your plans or your opinions.

Unit 1
Homework exercise

Group A

Write five questions about the <u>IELTS interview</u> from what you learned in Unit 1.

Unit 2
Exercise 16

Example:

Student 1: I live at home with my parents. My father is a businessman, and my mother is a housewife. I have an older brother. But he doesn't live with us. He lives with his <u>de facto</u> wife.

Student 2: I'm sorry, I don't know what 'de facto' means.

Student 1: Well, my brother and his wife aren't actually married – I mean, they didn't have a wedding. But they have lived together for five years, so it's really the same as if they were married. So they are 'de facto' husband and wife.

Student 2: I see. And are 'de facto' marriages common in your country?

Student 1: Oh, yes. Anyway, he's a teacher. And I also have a younger sister. She's studying in the States at the moment. She's really intelligent. She's studying for a PhD in education.

Unit 2
Exercise 27

Group A

Read the text below in which someone is describing a traditional, western, Christian wedding and add any further words to your lists in Exercise 26.

The clothes that people wear at an old-fashioned wedding are very important. The bride typically wears a long white dress with a veil, and she carries a bouquet of flowers. The groom generally wears morning dress – that's a grey three-piece suit, consisting of matching trousers, waistcoat and a jacket with tails – and a top hat of the same colour. The groom's closest friend usually acts as 'best man'; the best man's main job is to look after the wedding ring until the groom puts it on the bride's hand. There are often bridesmaids, who wear matching dresses in a pastel colour such as pale pink or lemon yellow. And sometimes there's a little page boy in a velvet suit. The bride customarily wears or carries 'something old, something new, something borrowed and something blue', but I'm not sure where this tradition comes from.

Unit 3
Exercise 8

Set 1

Departure time of next train	indirect question
Arrival time	'wh' question
Cost – single/return ticket	yes/no question
Need for seat reservation	tag question
Platform number	'wh' question
Buffet car/restaurant car	either/or question

Set 2

Departure time of next train	'wh' question'
Arrival time	'wh' question
Cost – single/return ticket	either/or question
Need for seat reservation	yes/no question
Platform number	indirect question
Buffet car/restaurant car	tag question

Set 3

Departure time of next train	'wh' question
Arrival time	indirect question
Cost – single/return ticket	tag question
Need for seat reservation	either/or question
Platform number	'wh' question
Buffet car/restaurant car	yes/no question

Unit 4
Exercise 2

Student A

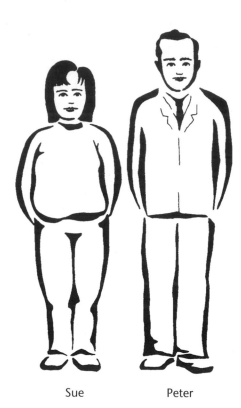

Sue   Peter

Unit 4.
Exercise 20

Group A

1 What do you enjoy doing in your free time? Discuss your hobbies and interests as a group and find out:
   • Who has the most unusual hobby?
   • Who has the largest number of hobbies?
   • Who spends the most time on their hobby/hobbies?
   • Whose hobby is the cheapest?
   • Whose hobby is the most expensive?

2 Think back five or ten years ago. Discuss what your hobbies and interests were then and find out:
   • Who still has exactly the same hobbies now?
   • Whose hobbies have changed most?
   • Why have people's hobbies changed or not changed?

What tense(s) did you use in Section 1 above? What tense(s) did you use in Section 2 above?

Find a partner from Group B. Ask them to report Group B's findings. As you listen to your partner, note down how often he or she uses the language of comparison that has been taught in this unit and how often he or she uses the structure:

'used to' + infinitive (e.g. I used to like, people used to play)
the present perfect

When your partner has finished, tell him or her what you noticed about his or her use of the language of comparison and 'used to'.

Unit 5
Exercise 12

A: In my opinion, classical music is boring.
B: Really? My view is that it can be really exciting.

A: From my point of view, cigarettes should be made illegal. I mean, scientists are always telling us that smoking causes all sorts of terrible diseases.
B: You're probably right. But the way I see it, many governments make a lot of money from the taxes they put on tobacco, so there's no way that they'll make smoking illegal.

Unit 6
Exercise 12

Subsequently, ...
In the end, ...
Then ...
The next stage is/was ...
Initially, ...
Finally, ...
Later on, ...
Having ...,
At first, ...
Next, ...
After that,
Shortly after ...,
After ...,
Shortly after that, ...
After a while, ...
Some time later, ...
Afterwards, ...

Unit 6
Homework exercise

Group A
Prepare questions to ask other students about the following topics:
a   The education system in his or her country, from primary school to university.

b The human rights record of his or her country; how and why it has changed over the years.
c How the student him or herself obtained a job in the past.
d The process by which rice is grown.
e The process of opening a bank account.

Think about how you would respond to such questions yourself.

Unit 7
Exercise 9

1 So, you're applying for residence in New Zealand. Why have you chosen to move to New Zealand?

GIVE A REASON/OPINION	....
PROVIDE SUPPORT FOR OPINION	....
GIVE ANOTHER REASON	....
GIVE EXAMPLE(S)	....

2 And what exactly are you planning to do in New Zealand – are you going to work or study, for example?

OUTLINE FUTURE PLAN	....
GIVE DETAILS OF PLAN	....
GIVE REASONS FOR PLAN	....

3 And what is your ambition for your future in New Zealand?

STATE AMBITION	....
GIVE DETAILS OF AMBITION	....
PROVIDE REASONS FOR AMBITION	....

Unit 7
Exercise 23

Group A

Work together to decide on some <u>answers</u> for the following prompt card. Try to include some alternative plans in your ideas.

PROMPT CARD

> The examiner has just completed a Master of Linguistics degree course. Ask the examiner questions about the following:
>
> - Results of the course
> - Whether s/he plans to go on holiday
> - Whether s/he plans to look for a job
> - The type of job s/he is interested in
> - The possibility for further studies – for example for a PhD
> - Long-term goals

Unit 8
Exercise 7

Question: What will you do if you are unsuccessful in getting the grade you need for New Zealand Residence purposes?

Unit 8
Exercise 15

Question: What will happen if you are unable to get the grade you need for New Zealand Residence purposes?

Unit 8
Exercise 16

Question: What problem(s) do you anticipate encountering in your life in a foreign country?

Unit 8
Exercise 20

Group A

You are going to answer a set of questions. In your answers, try to incorporate examples of the following functions (you can use examples of other functions too, but you MUST try and use the ones listed below). As a group, discuss all the language that you have learnt for expressing these functions:
- Expressing uncertainty
- Expressing opinions
- Giving reasons
- Hypothesising
- Expressing desire to do something
- Asking for clarification

Unit 8
Exercise 21

a What are your chances of getting the score you want in the IELTS examination?
b When can you become a New Zealand citizen?
c How will economic relations between your country and New Zealand change in the future? Why?
d How will political relations between your country and New Zealand change in the future? Why?
e What, if any, changes will there be to New Zealand immigration rules in the future?
f Will the number of people migrating from your country to New Zealand increase in the future?
g Why have you chosen to live in New Zealand?
h Will you return to your home country for holidays?

Unit 1
Exercise 4

Group B

The IELTS Interview

The IELTS speaking test consists of an 11 to 15 minute interview. The interview, which is recorded onto an audio cassette tape, consists of five different sections, which last varying lengths of time, namely:

Section 1	Introduction	1–2 minutes
Section 2	Extended discourse	3–4 minutes
Section 3	Elicitation	3–4 minutes
Section 4	Speculation and attitudes	3–4 minutes
Section 5	Conclusion	1 minute

Section 1 is usually quite relaxed and informal. You should greet the examiner, who will then ask a few general 'social conversation' questions, such as where you are from and how long you have been learning English. These questions are usually based on the Personal Details form that you complete when you register for the IELTS examination.

In section 2 of the interview, the interviewer may ask you to talk on such topics as your educational background, jobs you have held, your home and family, your hobbies and interests, your country (its geography, culture, education system, politics, economy, festivals, customs and climate, etc.), your home town (its population, transport system, attractions, industries and economy, etc.). When talking about these topics, the interviewer may ask you to give descriptions or provide general information; to describe a process or sequence of events; to compare and contrast two or more things; to state likes, dislikes and preferences; to express opinions; to give reasons for those likes/dislikes, preferences and opinions; to express interest in something; to express desire to do something.

In section 3 of the interview, you are expected to ask questions in order to obtain information from the examiner. You will be given a prompt card which outlines an imaginary situation and gives you some suggestions for questions that you could ask the interviewer. You should use a variety of question forms, not just the simple form, 'How about X?'

In section 4 of the interview, the examiner will ask you questions about the future, usually about your future plans and intentions – for example, what further studies you hope to follow, what personal or work-related ambitions you have, what problems you expect to have when studying or working in an English-speaking country, etc. You may also be asked to consider not only your own future, but the future for your country.

In Section 5, the examiner will conclude the interview. He or she may wish you luck, thank you and then say goodbye. You should respond naturally, according to what the examiner says.

Unit 1
Homework exercise

Group B
Write five questions about <u>this book</u> (*Language Passport*) from what you learned in Unit 1.

Unit 2
Exercise 27

Group B
Read the text below in which someone is describing a traditional, western, Christian wedding and add any further words to your lists in Exercise 26.

The wedding ceremony is held in a church and when it's finished, everyone takes photographs of the couple and their families, the bridesmaids and the best man – usually on the steps outside the church. And people throw confetti over the married couple. Then all the guests go to the reception to have something to eat and drink. At the end of the meal or buffet, family members make speeches and 'toast' the newly-married couple with champagne and wish them a long and happy life together. And there's a special wedding cake – a sort of rich fruit cake covered with white icing – often three or even four tiers high, which the newly-weds have to cut together, using one knife. Then, when the reception is all over, the bride and groom go off on honeymoon. There's a bit of a tradition to cover the newly-weds' car with balloons and lucky horseshoes, and to write things like 'just married' in lipstick on the car. I think the bride and groom generally stop the car as soon as they can and try to clean everything off so that people don't stare at them!

Unit 4
Exercise 2

Student B

Carole   Darren

Unit 4
Exercise 20

Group B

Discuss what forms of entertainment people in your country enjoy –
films, plays, musicals, live music, opera, TV, or radio. Find out:

1　What is the most popular form of entertainment among the
students in your group?
2　How much time do students in your group spend on different
forms of entertainment every week or month?
3　How frequently do students in your group enjoy their favourite
form of entertainment?
4　What is your parents' favourite form of entertainment now?
5　What do you think was your parents' favourite form of
entertainment when they were your age?
6　Why has popular entertainment changed or not changed over the
years?

What tense(s) did you use in questions 1–4 above? What tense(s) did
you use in questions 5 and 6 above?

Find a partner from Group A. Ask them to report Group A's findings. As you listen to your partner, note down how often he or she uses the language of comparison that has been taught in this unit and how often he or she uses:
- the past simple tense (e.g. I liked, people played)
- the present perfect tense (e.g. It has changed.)

When your partner has finished, tell him or her what you noticed about his or her use of the language of comparison and of the past simple and present perfect tenses.

Unit 6

Homework exercise

Group B
Prepare questions to ask other students about the following topics:
a A traditional instrument from his or her country and how it is played.
b The process by which the student him or herself has obtained a visa or permit to visit/study/live in another country.
c How people in his or her country obtain passports.
d The process of building a traditional house in his or her country.
e How formal business meetings are conducted.

Think about how you would respond to such questions yourself.

Unit 7

Exercise 23

Group B
Work together to decide on some <u>answers</u> for the following prompt card. Try to include some alternative plans in your ideas.

PROMPT CARD

The examiner is moving to live in another country. Ask the examiner questions about the following:

- The country s/he is moving to
- How long s/he plans to stay there
- Whether s/he has a job there
- What sort of job
- His/her family's plans – e.g. to join him or not

Unit 8
Exercise 20

Group B
You are going to answer a set of questions. In your answers, incorporate examples of the following functions (you can use examples of other functions too, but you MUST try and use the ones listed below). As a group, discuss all the language that you have learnt for expressing these functions:
- Expressing supposition
- Expressing non-comprehension
- Coping with difficult questions
- Comparing and contrasting
- Expressing likes and dislikes

Unit 8
Exercise 24

Revision board game

Equipment
For this game you need:
- A counter for each student
- Sufficient photocopies of the board for all students to play (three or four students per board)
- One dice per board and group of three or four students
- A pack of 'Function and Topic Cards'
- A pack of 'Language Cards'

Rules
1 Play with three or four people to a board.
2 Each player should have a counter.
3 Take it in turns to throw the dice and advance on the board according to the number you have thrown.
4 When you land on a 'function' (Description, Comparison, Sequence, Uncertainty or Reason), pick up two cards: a 'Function and Topic Card' for the function you have landed on and also the 'Language Card' for that function.
5 Show your cards to the other three players on your board and talk about your topic for 30 seconds or more, including as many of the language expressions as you can. The other players will decide if your 30 second talk was good enough. If not, you must miss a turn the next time!
6 The winner is the first person to reach 'The End'.
7 You must throw an exact number to land on 'The End'.
8 You cannot remain on the same square – you must move either backwards or forwards every time you throw the dice.

Function and Topic Cards (photocopy and cut out)
'Describe' Function and Topic Cards

✂

'DESCRIBE' F & T CARD
Describe a traditional dish from your country.

'DESCRIBE' F & T CARD
Describe the ethnic mix in your country.

'DESCRIBE' F & T CARD
Describe an important festival in your country.

'DESCRIBE' F & T CARD
Describe your home town.

'DESCRIBE' F & T CARD
Describe a traditional instrument from your country.

'DESCRIBE' F & T CARD
Describe the traditional architecture of your country.

'DESCRIBE' F & T CARD
Describe the education system in your country.

'DESCRIBE' F & T CARD
Describe an organisation you have worked for.

'DESCRIBE' F & T CARD
Describe the English language classes on this course.

'DESCRIBE' F & T CARD
Describe a traditional garment from your country.

'Sequence' Function and Topic Cards

'SEQUENCE' F & T CARD	'SEQUENCE' F & T CARD
Describe the process of obtaining a job in your country.	Describe the process of gaining entry to a university in your country.
'SEQUENCE' F & T CARD	'SEQUENCE' F & T CARD
Describe the process of obtaining a passport.	Describe the process of making a traditional dish from your country.
'SEQUENCE' F & T CARD	'SEQUENCE' F & T CARD
Describe the process of obtaining a driving licence in your country.	Describe your own education from primary school to tertiary institute.
'SEQUENCE' F & T CARD	'SEQUENCE' F & T CARD
Describe your working life from your first job until the present day.	Describe what you do on a typical day from when you get up until you go to bed again at night.
	'SEQUENCE' F & T CARD
	Describe how you learnt a sport or skill that you have.

'Compare' Function and Topic Cards

✂

| 'COMPARE' F & T CARD |
| Compare family life in your country and another country. |

| 'COMPARE' F & T CARD |
| Compare a traditional house in your country with a modern home in your country. |

| 'COMPARE' F & T CARD |
| Compare your home town with another town. |

| 'COMPARE' F & T CARD |
| Compare public transport in your home town with that in a very different town/city. |

| 'COMPARE' F & T CARD |
| Compare the climate in your country with the climate in another country. |

| 'COMPARE' F & T CARD |
| Compare this IELTS course with another English course you have done. |

| 'COMPARE' F & T CARD |
| Compare traffic in your home town with traffic in another town. |

| 'COMPARE' F & T CARD |
| Compare the roles of men and women in your country. |

| 'COMPARE' F & T CARD |
| Compare two forms of public transport (e.g. bus and train). |

| 'COMPARE' F & T CARD |
| Compare the advantages of public transport and cars. |

'Uncertainty' Function and Topic Cards

'UNCERTAINTY' F & T CARD
Discuss the future of
tourism in your
country.

'UNCERTAINTY' F & T CARD
Discuss social change
in your country
in the future.

'UNCERTAINTY' F & T CARD
Discuss some aspect of your
country's economy, politics
or international relations in
the future.

'UNCERTAINTY' F & T CARD
Talk about your
future career.

'UNCERTAINTY' F & T CARD
Talk about your future
personal life.

'UNCERTAINTY' F & T CARD
Discuss your chances of
'passing' the IELTS
examination!

'UNCERTAINTY' F & T CARD
Talk about the numbers of
students from your country
studying overseas.

'UNCERTAINTY' F & T CARD
Talk about the numbers of
overseas tourists visiting your
country in the future.

'Reasons' Function and Topic Cards

✂

'REASONS' F & T CARD Give reasons why you have chosen to study/live overseas.	**'REASONS' F & T CARD** Give reasons why you have chosen a particular country to study/live in.
'REASONS' F & T CARD Give reasons why you have chosen to take the IELTS examination.	**'REASONS' F & T CARD** Give reasons why you like or dislike a particular type of film, sport or book.
'REASONS' F & T CARD Give reasons why you want or don't want to do a particular job in the future.	**'REASONS' F & T CARD** Give reasons why the divorce rate has (or hasn't) increased in your country.
'REASONS' F & T CARD Give reasons why you would or wouldn't like to visit a particular country.	**'REASONS' F & T CARD** Give reasons why couples in your country have fewer (or more) children than in the past.

Language Cards (photocopy and cut out)

'Describe' Language Card

'DESCRIBE' LANGUAGE CARD

a great many/a large number of/not many/a few
various types/groups/forms
extremely common
highly popular
typical
the most frequent/frequently
X consists of

'Sequence' Language Card

'SEQUENCE' LANGUAGE CARD

initially
subsequently
later on
shortly after that
having …'ed
the next stage
finally
after …'ing
in the end
after a while
until
while

'Compare' Language Card

'COMPARE' LANGUAGE CARD

totally different/slightly different/very similar/
    exactly the same
with regard to/with respect to/as regards
similarly/likewise/both A and B
in contrast/on the other hand
whereas/while
much ...er than/less ...er than
slightly ...er than/a little ...er than

'Uncertainty' Language Card

'UNCERTAINTY' LANGUAGE CARD

It's difficult to say/I'm not altogether certain/It
    remains to be seen
I'm not too sure/I'm not entirely sure
It's possible that ...
I guess/I imagine/I suppose/I suspect
It's impossible to know ...
perhaps/maybe
If X, Y will/If X, Y would
I hope/I expect/I anticipate

'Reasons' Language Card

'REASONS' LANGUAGE CARD

The primary reason/The main reason/An
   important reason/The key factor
One reason/One factor
Another reason/Another factor
A further reason/A further factor
In my opinion/From my point of view/It seems to
   me that
The way I see it/As I see it/My view is that
   fond of/keen on/interested in/attracted to
X doesn't appeal to Y/X doesn't interest Y

START
FINISH

REASONS

COMPARISONS

DESCRIPTION

THROW AGAIN!

COMPARISONS

UNCERTAINTY

Revision
Game Board

REASONS

SEQUENCE

SEQUENCE

REASONS

CHOOSE ANY
FUNCTION

UNCERTAINTY

DESCRIPTION

COMPARISON

GO BACK TO
THE START!

Tapescripts

Tapescript 1

Unit 1
Exercise 11

Organiser:	. . . alright, so I've got your name and address. Now ... now for your date of birth. When were you born?
Student:	April 5th, 1972.
Organiser:	5th April, '72. And you're female. Now. Oh, where are you from?
Student:	Taiwan.
Organiser:	OK. Oh, so, is your mother tongue Chinese?
Student:	Yes, that's right.
Organiser:	Right, and ... What do you do?
Student:	My job, you mean?
Organiser:	Mmm, yes.
Student:	I'm a student.
Organiser:	Student. Now, um ... Are you taking the IELTS test for further education, for work purposes or for personal reasons?
Student:	Further education.
Organiser:	Uh huh. Right and oh, what are you hoping to study?
Student:	After I do the IELTS test?
Organiser:	Yes.
Student:	A certificate in hospitality and tourism.
Organiser:	Right. So that's a vocational training programme, isn't it?
Student:	Yes.
Organiser:	Good. Right. And, er, which institution are you applying to?
Student:	AIT – Auckland Institute of Technology.
Organiser:	Um, and what level of education have you completed – secondary school up to 16 years, secondary between 16 and 19 years of age, university degree or postgraduate?
Student:	I finished secondary school when I was 18.
Organiser:	Uh, huh. Right. Um ... and how long have you been studying English?
Student:	Gosh, I'm not sure. Oh, I suppose it's been about six years.
Organiser:	Six years. Fine. OK. Well, that's everything on the form, so now all we need to do is . . .

Tapescript 2

Unit 1
Exercise 13

a Where are you **from**?
b Is your mother tongue Chin**ese**?
c What do you **do**?
d Are you taking the IELTS test for further edu**ca**tion, for **work** purposes or for **per**sonal reasons?
e Which institution are you a**pply**ing to?
f How **long** have you been **stu**dying **Eng**lish?

Tapescript 3

Unit 1
Exercise 14

a What's your **sur**name?
b What's your **fir**st name?
c Some varieties of English, including British English have the stress:
   Can you give me your add**ress**, please?
   Other varieties of English, including American English have the stress: Can you give me your **ad**dress, please?
d When were you **born**?
e Could you tell me what **sub**ject you are going to study?
f What **le**vel of education have you completed?

Tapescript 4

Unit 1
Exercise 18

Interviewer: Um … Please say your name in full for me.
Interviewee: Yes. It's Liu Jiang Mei.
Interviewer: Er … And what would you like me to call you?
Interviewee: Well, you could call me 'May'. That's what most of my friends call me because it's easier than 'Jiang Mei'.
Interviewer: Fine. Yes. Well, May, according to your form, you live in Staines Road here in Christchurch.
Interviewee: Yes, that's right.
Interviewer: Um … In a house or a flat?
Interviewee: A flat. I share a flat with a couple of friends.
Interviewer: I see. And you're from Taiwan?
Interviewee: Yes.
Interviewer: Um … Whereabouts in Taiwan?
Interviewee: From Taipei, the capital.
Interviewer: Right. Um … And your first language is Chinese, of course. Um … But do you speak any other languages?
Interviewee: No. Not apart from English, that is.
Interviewer: And it says here that you're a student.
Interviewee: Yes.
Interviewer: Studying English, you mean?
Interviewee: Yes. I've been studying here in Christchurch for the past six months.
Interviewer: Right, so, um … Now you say you're, you're intending to study on a vocational training course.

Interviewee:	Mmm, yes.
Interviewer:	What particular field?
Interviewee:	Tourism. I want to work in the tourist industry back home in Taiwan.
Interviewer:	Mm. But you're taking this IELTS exam to go on to further studies, I see.
Interviewee:	Yes. I'm hoping to follow a course in tourism at … um … Lincoln University.
Interviewer:	Is that an undergraduate or … or a postgraduate course?
Interviewee:	Er … Undergraduate. It's a three-year course leading to a Bachelor's degree.
Interviewer:	Alright, well, going back to . . .

Tapescript 5

Unit 1
Exercise 23

Section 1

(knock on the door)

Interviewer:	Hello, come on in.
Interviewee:	Thank you. Er … should I close the door?
Interviewer:	Yes, yes please. And take a seat.
Interviewee:	Thanks.
Interviewer:	Um … My name's Susan and I'm your interviewer for today.
Interviewee:	Pleased to meet you.

Section 5

Interviewee:	and ultimately, I hope to be able to set up my own tour guide operation, you know, … um … catering for English-speaking tourists.
Interviewer:	I see. Um … well, I think we'll end the interview there. So, um … I wish you luck with your plans …
Interviewee:	Thank you.
Interviewer:	And … and are you on holiday now?
Interviewee:	Yes … um … My English course finished yesterday.
Interviewer:	Oh, well, I imagine you'll be feeling more relaxed now that you've finished the IELTS examination.
Interviewee:	Oh, yes. Yes, definitely.
Interviewer:	Well, it's been nice meeting you, then. Goodbye.
Interviewee:	Goodbye. And thank you.

Tapescript 6

Unit 2
Exercises 6 and 7

I suppose my country has a fairly moderate climate. There are four distinct seasons: spring, summer, autumn and winter. The winter isn't very cold – it's generally quite mild; the temperatures rarely fall below five degrees centigrade. But it's also quite wet in winter and very cloudy and dull. Cold winds blow across the country from the north quite often in spring and autumn, but the summer is generally warm, with temperatures around, say, 20 to 26 degrees centigrade and plenty of sunshine. Even so, when it rains in summer the temperatures can drop to a cool 15 degrees, but they rise quickly again when the clouds clear.

Tapescript 7

Unit 2
Exercise 12

Asking the interviewer to repeat
I'm **sorry**, could you s**ay** that a**gain**?
I'm **sorry**, I **did**n't quite **cat**ch that.
Sorry, could you re**peat** that?
Sorry, could you re**peat** your **que**stion?

Expressing non-comprehension
What does 'de **fa**cto' mean?
I **don't** know what 'de **fa**cto' means.
I'm afraid I **do**n't quite under**stand** what you **mean**.

Tapescript 8

Unit 2
Exercise 14

Interviewer:	So both your brothers are toddlers?
Interviewer:	Tell me about your family. [Interviewer's voice becomes inaudible at the end.]
Interviewer:	How does your father earn his livelihood?
Interviewer:	How long have your parents been estranged?
Interviewer:	Which country were your forebears from?
Interviewer:	And how many of you live at home? [Interviewer's voice masked by noise in the middle of the sentence.]
Interviewer:	Would you say your upbringing was a traditional one?
Interviewer:	Is it common for aunts and uncles to help rear each others children?
Interviewer:	So which country do you officially reside in?

Tapescript 9

Unit 2
Exercise 19

1 I've forgotten the English name for it, but ... well it's a fruit – not a soft fruit – it's quite hard and crisp. Um ... it's sort of round in shape and it's about the size of a tennis ball – maybe, maybe a little bigger. It's sometimes green, sometimes red on the outside and sort of white on the inside. And, it grows on trees. Um, it's got seeds in the centre. And, well, some people peel the skin off, you know, before they eat it.

2 I can't remember what it's called. It's a vegetable. It's long and thin and hard, and it grows underground. It's an orange colour and it's got feathery green leaves that come out of the top. People say that it can help you see in the dark. And rabbits like it. It's quite sweet.

3 I don't know the name for it but it's something sweet that you eat at the end of a meal. It's got fruit like blackberries on the bottom and then there's a mixture of flour and butter and sugar on the top that's like sand or lots of tiny balls. People eat it hot with custard, cream or ice cream.

4 The name escapes me at the moment, but it's a ... a grain, like rice. But it doesn't grow in water, as rice does. I think it's grown a lot in Europe and the United States and it gets to be about half a metre high and ... oh, it's used for making bread and pizzas and things like that.

Tapescript 10

**Unit 3
Exercise 5**

Interviewee:	I wonder if I could ask you some questions about a student travelcard.
Interviewer:	Mmm, yes, of course. Well, what would you like to know?
Interviewee:	How much does it cost?
Interviewer:	Um ... it's $50.
Interviewee:	How long is it valid for?
Interviewer:	Oh ... just a year. Um ... you have to renew it each year that you are a student.
Interviewee:	Does it just cover buses or can I use it for trains and for air travel?
Interviewer:	Um ... you can use it for intercity coach and rail travel. But not for buses around town or for plane journeys, I'm afraid.
Interviewee:	Can you tell me about the benefits that having a travelcard would give me?
Interviewer:	Sure. Um ... well ... you get 10% off both single and return tickets for coach or train travel.
Interviewee:	Are there any restrictions?
Interviewer:	Er ... yes, yes. You can only use it for yourself; um ... of course, you can't lend it to a friend or buy tickets for friends with it either.
Interviewee:	Where can I get a travelcard?
Interviewer:	Um ... at the Students' Union office here on campus.
Interviewee:	I'll need to show them some form of identification, won't I?
Interviewer:	Oh, yes. Um ... you'll need to take a ... your student card with you, you know, to prove you are eligible for a student travelcard.
Interviewee:	Do I have to take any other documents with me?
Interviewer:	Um ... Just a passport size photograph.
Interviewee:	Thanks for the information.

Tapescript 11

Unit 3
Exercise 10

a Where can I get a **travel**card, please?

b Can I use it for **trains**?

c Can you tell me what the **ben**efits are?

d I'll need to show them some form of identif**ic**ation, **won't** I?

e Do I pay **now** or later?

f Does it just cover **bus**es?

g How long is it **val**id for?

h Are there any res**tric**tions?

i My **frien**ds can't use it, **can** they?

j Is it valid for a **year** or **long**er?

k How much does it **cost**?

l Do you know where I can **buy** one?

Tapescript 12

Unit 3
Exercise 14

Interviewee: Er ... I wonder if I could ask you some questions about a student travelcard?

Interviewer: Mmm. Yes, of course. What would you like to know?

Interviewee: Well, first of all, how much does it cost?

Interviewer: Er ... it's $50.

Interviewee: Oh, it's quite cheap, then. But ... um how long is it valid for?

Interviewer: Er ... just a year. Um ... you have to renew it each year that you are a student.

Interviewee: I see; so it's $50 per year. And does it cover just buses or can I use it for trains and for air travel?

Interviewer: Um ... you can use it for intercity coach and rail travel. Um ... not for buses around town or ... or for plane journeys, I'm afraid.

Interviewee: Mmm, that's a pity. Um ... can you tell me about the benefits that having a travelcard would give me?

Interviewer: Oh, sure. Um ... you get 10% off both single and return tickets for coach or train travel.

Interviewee: Yeah, 10%? That's not bad. Are there any um ... restrictions?

Interviewer: Yes ... um ... you can only use it for yourself; um ... you can't lend it to a friend or buy tickets for friends with it.

Interviewee: No, no. Of course not. So, um, where can I get a travelcard?

Interviewer: Er ... at the Students' Union office here on campus.

Interviewee: Oh, good. That's handy. Um ... I'll need to show them some form of identification, won't I?

Interviewer:	Yes ... um ... you'll need to take your student card with you, to prove that you are eligible for a Student Travelcard
Interviewee:	Just my student card or do I have to take any other documents with me?
Interviewer:	Um ... just a passport size photograph.
Interviewee:	Well, it sounds a pretty good deal really. Thanks ... thanks for the information.

Tapescript 13

Unit 4
Exercise 14

Group 1 – Emphasising similarities

similarly
both **A** and **B** have/are
likewise
as in **A**, so in **Y** there is/are

Group 2 – Emphasising differences

in **con**trast
where**as**
on the **o**ther hand
while

Tapescript 14

Unit 4
Exercise 17

Education in Sweden and the UK

Sweden and the UK have ... well ... rather ... yeah, rather different approaches to education ... well, at least as regards ... um ... the age at which schooling begins ... um ... so, while children in the UK must attend primary school from the age of five ... um ... Swedish children start primary school at the age of eight. Um ... yeah ... and another difference ... er ... another difference is the age at which children start their secondary schooling. So pupils in Sweden spend approximately ... um ... two years at a lower secondary school, that's from the ages of 14 to 16 ... um ... whereas their UK counterparts begin to study at secondary school at 12 years of age. Um ... and at 16 ... er ... Swedish students move from a lower secondary school to an upper secondary school. On the other hand, in the UK, students may choose to stay on at their secondary school from 16 to 18 or, alternatively, they ... they can transfer to a sixth-form college.

Yeah, but the ... there are, however, ... there are similarities. Yeah, before primary school, Swedish children may attend the optional preschools; and likewise, the UK has optional pre-primary schooling in the form of nursery schools. And furthermore, both Sweden and the UK have compulsory schooling throughout primary school and at secondary school until 16 years of age. Um ... yeah ... and also, as in Sweden, so in the UK the optional later secondary phase usually ends around the age of 18.

Tapescript 15

Unit 4
Exercise 21

Crime

In recent years there has been an overall increase in crime. Certain types of crime have become more common, whilst others have declined. Mugging, for example, has risen sharply – whereas around 2000 people were attacked and robbed in the street last year, this year the figure reached almost 2800. Similarly, the number of cases of house burglary and of theft from cars has grown. So, too, has the incidence of vandalism, particularly such things as damage to public phone boxes, to road and street signs, and to street lights. In contrast, some violent crimes, such as murder, manslaughter and sexual attacks, have declined, as has corruption, fraud and forgery. Drinking and driving has also fallen to a much lower level as a result of the new police campaign.

Politics

Over the last 30 years the country has seen great changes in its political system. A military government was in power for ... for many years, but this was replaced in 1981 by a democratic parliamentary system and, well, in that year a left-wing socialist government was elected. There are now three main parties: that's the socialist People's Party, the right-wing National Party and the central Liberal Democratic Party. And there are around 400 members of parliament, I think. At the moment, the Liberal Democrats have slightly more MPs than any other party. And their leader, the prime minister of the country, is a woman. There are, in fact, four female ministers in the government, but there are still far more male politicians than female.

Marriage and divorce

Up to about ... um ... 40 years ago, the average marriage age in my country was 20 and couples were married for life because ... um ... divorce was illegal. Things are totally different now, particularly with regard to ... um ... marriage age. It's risen ... um ... considerably and it is now at around 28. Large numbers of people now live together without getting married. Some couples marry when they decide to have children, but there are also many ... er ... illegitimate babies born to couples who never get married, and there is no ... um ... stigma now to having illegitimate children. About one in three marriages break down and end in divorce, and there are now slightly more children living in one-parent families than in the ... um ... traditional nuclear families. When parents separate, the children usually remain with the mother and the father pays ... um ... maintenance money to the mother.

Tapescript 16

Unit 5
Exercise 6

I enjoy skiing.
I'm **keen** on skiing.
I'm **fond** of skiing.
I'm not **interested** in skiing.
I don't **go** for skiing.
I'm not **into** skiing.

Tapescript 17

Unit 5
Exercise 11

Expressing an opinion
From **my** point of view …
As **I** see it …
In **my** opinion …
It seems to **me** that …
My view is that …
The way **I** see it …

Tapescript 18

Unit 5
Exercises 14
and 19

I'd like to be a hotel receptionist because I enjoy meeting people. Er
… the way I see it, I'd make a good receptionist because I particularly
like meeting people from different countries. And I've got a really
friendly manner – or so my friends tell me – and on top of that I'm
very patient. Another reason why I believe it would suit me is that I
always like to look neat and tidy – I really take care of my
appearance, and that's important for a receptionist. And, well, finally
it seems to me that I also have the right skills and qualifications – I
speak three languages, I can type a little and I have a certificate in
hospitality and tourism. So, all-in-all, I feel it's the right job for me
and that I'd be good at it. I'm really keen on the idea of getting a
position with an international chain of hotels and then moving
round the world from country to country working for the same
organisation.

Tapescript 19

Unit 5
Exercise 21

b
I pre**fer** to …
I'd **rather** …
I'm **more in**terested in …
… ap**peals** to me more.
I'm **more** at**trac**ted to …
… **in**terests me more.

c
I much prefer to …
I'd much rather …
I'm much more interested in …

… appeals to me much more.
I'm much more attracted to …
… interests me much more.

Tapescript 20

Unit 5
Exercise 26

A: In my home town, the local government is creating lots of cycle tracks all round the city to encourage people to use bicycles instead of cars to get to work.

B: Mmm. Yes. And what do you think about that?

A: Well, to my mind, bikes are the modern answer to the problems of city life.

B: The modern answer? How do you mean?

A: Well, for example, they take up very little space. That solves a number of problems that most modern cities suffer from, including really reducing traffic jams, making parking space easier to find and … er … meaning people who live in small city flats can store them easily.

B: Mmm. I take your point. Mmm.

A: And that's not all. More bicycles mean lower taxes.

B: I'm afraid I don't follow you.

A: Well, the tax money that people pay and that is spent on maintaining and repairing roads is a case in point. Because bicycles are a great deal lighter than cars and buses, roads are not damaged as much by bikes. As a result, the amount of money we pay in tax for road repairs can be expected to go down.

B: Mmm. Right. Mmm.

A: To my mind, you'd also see a difference in medical expenses.

B: Er … could you explain what you mean about a difference in medical expenses?

A: Well, cycling is really good for your health. Heart disease, for instance, can be prevented by taking regular exercise, like cycling to work every day. Heart disease is really one of the problems of modern city life that I mentioned before, isn't it? So, if we can improve the health of people living in the city, we can reduce the amount of tax money spent on hospitals, medicines, etc.

B: Yes, yes, maybe so. You could be right.

Tapescript 21

Unit 6
Exercise 1

Honey cake

OK. You start by beating some eggs in a blender. And … um … at the same time you cut the butter into small pieces and then use a … um … wooden spoon to cream it in a bowl. When that's done, you beat the honey in with the butter. And after a while, when the honey and butter mixture is nice and light and liquid, you mix in the flour and the beaten eggs. As soon as that's done, you gently stir in some sultanas and then immediately pour the mixture into a cake tin and bake the cake for ... oh ... about ... um ... 20–25 minutes in a moderately hot oven.

French onion soup

Well, let me see ... you slice a couple of onions into thin rings and while you are doing that you heat up some oil in a frying pan. And ... er ... then when the oil is moderately hot, you fry the onion rings for about 15 minutes, stirring them all the time. And ... er ... at the same time, you heat a litre of vegetable stock in a pan. OK, so when the onions are cooked, you sprinkle them with a little salt and pepper and, after a few seconds, you stir them into the stock. You heat that mixture until it boils and then you reduce the heat and simmer it for about, say, 15 minutes. Meanwhile, you toast some slices of bread. And as soon as they are ready, you rub them with garlic and put them in the bottom of a dish. OK. Immediately after that you pour the onion soup over the toast and sprinkle grated cheese onto the soup. And the dish then goes under a grill and you grill the top of the soup until the cheese has melted and is bubbling. It's yummy, eh? It's really nice.

Tapescript 22

Unit 6
Exercise 13

Subsequently, ...
In the **end**, ...
Then ...
The **next** stage is/was ...
Initially, ...
Finally, ...
Later **on**, ...
Having ...,
At **first**, ...
Next, ...
After **that**,
Shortly after ...,
After ...,
Shortly after **that**, ...
After a **while**, ...
Some time **later**, ...
Afterwards, ...

Tapescript 23

Unit 6
Exercise 20

Text 1

Interviewer:	Um ... what would you say are the main differences um ... between your country and the UK?
Interviewee:	Um, I'm not sure.

Interviewer:	Ah ... well, what about food – how different is that?
Interviewee:	Oh, very different.
Interviewer:	Yes? Um ... in what ways?
Interviewee:	[pause] We eat a great deal of rice, whereas in the UK the staple is bread or potatoes.
Interviewer:	Uh huh. And any other differences?
Interviewee:	Er ... I'm sorry ... er ... I haven't thought about it.
Interviewer:	Alright ... um ... well, you said earlier that ... er ... a lot of young people in your country are unemployed.
Interviewee:	Yeah.
Interviewer:	Er ... why is that?
Interviewee:	I don't know.
Interviewer:	No idea?
Interviewee:	No. Er ... I haven't studied this subject.
Interviewer:	OK. Well, I wonder if it could be related to the economy or to population?
Interviewee:	Yes. Er ... our economy has suffered in recent years. And the population has increased so there aren't enough jobs.

Text 2

Interviewer:	So, what would you say are the main differences between your country and the UK?
Interviewee:	Oh ... um ... that's an interesting question. The main differences? Food – yes, you could say food is one.
Interviewer:	OK, and in what ways is it different?
Interviewee:	Um ... oh ... well … Well, for example, in my country we eat a great deal of rice, whereas in the UK the staple is ... um ... bread or potatoes.
Interviewer:	Mmmm ... mmm ... er ... and any other differences?
Interviewee:	I ... I'm sure there are, but just at the moment I can't think of any. I'm sorry.
Interviewer:	Alright. Um ... well ... you said earlier that a lot of young people in your country are unemployed.
Interviewee:	Yes.
Interviewer:	Um ... why is that?
Interviewee:	Um ... oh ... that's a good question. To be honest, I'm not very sure why there are a lot of unemployed young people, um ... oh ... but perhaps one reason could be that our economy has suffered in recent years. Um ... another reason may be that the population has increased and there aren't enough jobs for everyone. As I say, I'm not too sure of the reasons, but it is a serious problem because of ... well, because of the results.
Interviewer:	Results?

Interviewee:	Yeah. It's caused an increase in crime and also in the suicide rate among young people. Well, like in many cities now, there are large numbers of young people ...

Tapescript 24

**Unit 7
Exercise 6**

Dialogue 1

Interviewer:	Um ... on your CV, you state that you're applying for a course in accountancy. Um ... why have you chosen that particular field of study?
Student:	Er ... I like it. When I was a student at high school, I was good at it. I always got high marks in my exams. And I think an accountancy qualification will help me to get a good job later. People always need accountants and you can earn a lot of money as an accountant.
Interviewer:	I see. Um ... and what exactly will you do after you complete your accountancy course?
Student:	Er ... I'm not sure. I think I'd like to try and find a job in the accounts department of a big company like a multinational or an international company or something, but I don't know, really. I haven't decided yet.
Interviewer:	Mmm. And what is your ambition?
Student:	To be a big businessman. You know, have my own accountancy company with a big staff, or something like that, and make a lot of money. I reckon that'd be great.

Dialogue 2

Interviewer:	According to your CV, you're ... um ... going to study hospitality and tourism. Um ... why have you chosen that particular subject?
Student:	I ... I believe a qualification in hospitality and tourism will provide me with the ... um ... necessary skills for a job in the hotel industry.
Interviewer:	I see. Um ... and what will you do after you complete your hospitality and tourism course?
Student:	Um ... I intend to return home and I'll probably apply for a position with an international chain of hotels.
Interviewer:	Um ... and what is your ambition?
Student:	Ultimately, I plan on becoming a hotel manager.

Tapescript 25

Unit 7
Exercise 13

Group 1: could, might, may
Group 2: **op**tion, al**ter**native, possi**bil**ity, choice, po**ten**tial
Group 3: al**ter**natively, on the **oth**er hand, as an al**ter**native, or

Tapescript 26

Unit 7
Exercises 15 and 16

After completing my university course, I intend to return home and look for work. At the moment I'm not entirely sure what I'll do; I may apply for a post in an import-export business, ideally working in some way that I can use my English language skills. Er ... alternatively, I could take up a job in my father's firm – he has a business manufacturing electrical components. One option would be to start in a junior position and learn about the business by working my way up through the different departments in the company. On the other hand, I might begin work as a sales person in order to gain experience in marketing because my ... er ... ultimate aim is to set up an export division for my father's firm and sell the company's products overseas.

Tapescript 27

Unit 7
Exercise 18

A **dream** of mine is to to ...
I'm **fas**cinated by ...
I'm **real**ly **in**terested in ...
My **dream** is to ...
I'd **love** to ...
I find X **real**ly **in**teresting.
I think X is **ab**solutely **fas**cinating
I'd **real**ly like to ...
I'm in**trig**ued by ...
I have a **real** de**sire** to
X **real**ly ap**peals** to me.

Tapescript 28

Unit 7
Exercise 19

Interviewer: Do you have any particular personal ambitions?
Interviewee: Personal ambitions? Well, yes, I suppose I do, actually. I'd really like to visit Lhasa – you know, the capital of Tibet. It's about 3500 metres high, up in the Himalayan mountains. I'm fascinated by Tibet and by the Tibetan Buddhist religion and I'd love to see the monasteries in Lhasa, and the Tibetan pilgrims who go there. And another ambition of mine is to speak Samoan fluently. I'm really interested in learning languages – I can speak three quite well – and there's something particularly beautiful about the sound of the Samoan language – I find the

Samoan accent really attractive. So I'd love to be able to speak it well, you know, and with a good accent.

Tapescript 29

Unit 8
Exercise 9

Uncertainty
I'm not too **sure** what/who/where/when/how/why …
I'm not entirely **sure**.
I'm not altogether **cer**tain.
It's **diffi**cult to **say** what/who/where/when/how/why …
It's **diffi**cult to **know** what/who/where/when/how/why …
It re**mains** to be **seen** what/who/where/when/how/why …

Supposition
I i**ma**gine …
I guess …
I sus**pect** …
I sup**pose** …

Possibility
I may …..
I could …..
I might …..
Per**haps** …..
Maybe …..
It's **pos**sible that …..

Tapescript 30

Unit 8
Exercise 11

Interviewer: So, what problems do you anticipate encountering in your future studies at university?

Interviewee: Well, I expect I'll have a number of problems … um … both academically and socially, really. But I suppose the biggest hurdle could be getting to know people. I … I feel fairly confident about my ability to cope with my studies and … and the academic demands of the course, but I'm not altogether certain if … well … I'll find it easy to make friends with other students. I imagine I'll get to know the other overseas students quite quickly through the International Students' Club, but … ah, well, it remains to be seen if I'll get to know local students – you know, native English speakers – quite so easily. Perhaps I'm worrying unnecessarily, but I think I may find it difficult to talk to them and … um … well, you know, become friends with them.

Interviewer:	Why do you think it is so difficult for overseas students to make friends with native speakers?
Interviewee:	What makes it so difficult? Well, I suspect the primary reason is the language barrier. Um ... my formal English is of a high standard and that will help me with my academic work, but ... oh ... it seems to me that in order to socialise with other students I really need ... um ... informal, colloquial English. And another factor is accent; I'm not sure that I'll understand all the different English accents of the students. But, in my opinion, in addition to language problems, there's the ... um ... cultural gap. I believe that cultural differences may be a further reason why it's so difficult for overseas and native speaker students to ... um ... well, really get to know each other.
Interviewer:	Mmm. How do you think you could try to ... to actually overcome the difficulty of making friends with native speaker students?
Interviewee:	That's a good question. I'm not entirely sure, but ... well, I guess the best approach is to try and start talking about course work at maybe the end of a lecture or a tutorial; and then when I've broken the ice in that way, maybe I could suggest going for a cup of tea or coffee. And over coffee we might chat about other things – you know, I ... I could start by asking them questions about where they're from and so on. I know I can manage that sort of social chat, but it's difficult to know how to continue sometimes, really. I suppose another way would be to join a club – like a tennis club or a photography club – because that immediately gives you something to talk about, you know, to the other people in the club. It gives you ... um ... an interest in common that you can start from.

Answers

Unit 1
Exercise 6

Section 1	greeting and introducing yourself; providing personal information
Section 2	talking on a familiar topic (about your background or your experiences)
Section 3	asking questions in a role play
Section 4	expressing plans and hopes for the future
Section 5	saying goodbye

Exercise 7

The answers can be found in the Map of the Book.

Section 1	Unit(s) 1 (+ 6)
Section 2	Unit(s) 2, 4, 5, 6, 8 (+ 1 and 7)
Section 3	Unit(s) 1, 3, 8 (+ 4, 5, 6 and 7)
Section 4	Unit(s) 5, 6, 7, 8 (+ 1, 2 and 4)
Section 5	Unit(s) 1 (+ 2, 6 and 8)

Exercise 9

a Unit 2 'Explaining unknown words'
b Unit 5 'Giving reasons'
c Unit 6 'Using hesitation devices'
d Unit 6 'Coping with difficult questions'
e Unit 2 'Expressing non-comprehension'
f Unit 2 'Asking for repetition'
g Unit 5 'Asking for clarification'

Exercise 10

a True
b False. It is called your 'mother tongue'.
c True
d True
e False. 'To take a test' means 'to do a test' or 'to sit a test'.
f False. 'To complete' means 'to finish'.
g True

Exercise 17

a greeting and introducing yourself; providing personal information/ answering 'social conversation' questions
b 1–2 minutes.

Exercise 22

a Saying goodbye
b 1 minute

Unit 2
Exercise 1

Topics: your educational background, your jobs, your home, your family, your hobbies and interests, your country (geography, culture, education system, politics, economy, festivals, customs, climate), your home town (population, transport system, attractions, industries and economy).

Exercise 2

Functions: describing things and giving general information; describing a process of a sequence of events; comparing and contrasting; stating likes and dislikes; stating preferences; expressing opinions; giving reasons for likes/ dislikes, preferences and opinions; expressing interest in something; expressing desire to do something.

Exercise 3

In the Map of the Book or in Unit 2 itself (the headings and subheadings).

Topics: your family, your country – climate, culture (language, ethnic mix, religion, food), your country – customs (festivals, wedding ceremonies), your home town (population, attractions, industries and economy).
(NB Other topics are covered in later units.)

Functions: describing things/giving general information.
(NB Other functions are covered in later units.)

Exercise 4

1 Primarily the present simple tense (the present perfect and past tenses may also be relevant at times).

2 Comparing and contrasting   Unit 4
Expressing desire to do something   Unit 7
Expressing likes and dislikes   Unit 5
Expressing interest in something   Unit 7
Expressing preferences   Unit 5
Describing a sequence of events   Unit 6
Expressing opinions   Unit 5
Giving reasons   Units 5, 7 and 8

3 Dealing with vocabulary problems (expressing non-comprehension, explaining unknown words); asking for repetition.

Exercise 5

There are many possible answers to this question. One possibility is:

Adjectives – types of climate	Nouns – types of weather
extreme	snow
moderate	sunshine
alpine	rain
tropical	clouds
equatorial	winds
sub-tropical	

Adjectives – types of weather		Seasons
humid	sunny	spring
dry	cloudy	summer
hot	dull	autumn
cold		winter
cool		wet
mild		dry
warm		monsoon

Exercise 6

a moderate; spring; summer; autumn; winter; cold; mild; wet; cloudy; dull; winds; warm; sunshine; (rain – used as a verb); cool; clouds.

Exercise 11

a express non-comprehension
b ask the interviewer to repeat him/herself

Exercise 18
There are many different ways, including:
Describe it.
Give a definition.
Draw it.
Give an example.
Describe a situation.
Mime it.

Exercise 19
1 an apple
2 a carrot

3 fruit crumble
4 wheat

Exercise 20
size 1, 3, 4
cultivation 1, 2, 4
ingredients 3
shape 1, 2, 4
colour 1, 2

taste 2, 3
accompanying food 3
uses 2 (?), 4
texture 1, 2, 3

Exercise 23
a Christmas
b Guy Fawkes Night
c Remembrance Day
d Christmas
e Guy Fawkes Night

f Christmas
g Christmas
h Guy Fawkes Night
i Remembrance Day

Homework
Exercise A

Text 1

Economy	… it used to be a major port and it was also important for heavy industries such as ship building and car manufacturing.
	…the main source of employment is probably the service industries, things like insurance and banking and so on.
Population	around three quarters of a million people.
Location	…it's in the north west of England, about 250 miles from London.
Size	It's a large city.
Attractive features	..some lovely old buildings.
	the people are really friendly and have a great sense of humour.

Text 2

Economy	main shopping centre for the South Island.
	… lots of small manufacturing companies producing such things as clothing, footwear and electrical goods.
Population	300 000
Location	It's on the east coast of the South Island and it's not far from the Southern Alps – the main mountain range in the South Island.
Size	…the third largest city in New Zealand.
Attractive features	…all the parks and beautiful gardens.
	…a cultural centre too, with plenty of cinemas, theatres and art galleries.

Unit 3
Exercise 2
a Section 3
b your ability to make different question forms and to respond to the information that the interviewer gives you.

Exercise 3	1 'wh' questions (who, what, how, why, when, where)
	2 yes/no questions
	3 either/or questions
	4 indirect questions
	5 'how about' questions
	6 tag questions
	7 statements with 'question' intonation

The 'how about' question type should not be used more than once because it is too easy a question form.

Exercises 5 and 7

1   How much does it cost? – 'wh' question
2   How long is it valid for? – 'wh' question
3   Does it just cover buses or can I use it for trains and for air travel? – either/or question
4   Can you tell me about the benefits that having a travelcard would give me? – indirect question
5   Are there any restrictions? – Yes/no question
6   Where can I get a travelcard? – 'wh' question
7   I'll need to show them some form of identification, won't I? – tag question
8   Do I have to take any other documents with me? – Yes/no question

Exercise 10

1   There is more than one possible stress pattern, but a common stress pattern for each sentence is shown in the tapescript.

2   There is more than one possible intonation pattern, but a common intonation pattern for each sentence is given in the tapescript.

3   Intonation patterns depend on context, but commonly
    a   'wh' questions have falling intonation.
    b   yes/no questions have rising intonation.
    c   tag questions have falling intonation when the speaker is checking an idea, and rising intonation when the speaker is unsure of the answer.
    d   either/or questions have rising intonation on the first option and falling intonation on the second option.
    e   indirect questions have falling intonation.

Exercise 13

The student makes no response to the information that the interviewer gives in answer to his questions.

Exercise 19

Many of the questions would be in the past simple tense; one or two would probably use the form 'going to' to talk about the future. In contrast, earlier prompt card activities would have required only the use of the present simple tense.

Exercise 20

a   The question is an indirect question, so the form should be: Can I ask what the competition involved?
b   The competition has finished, so the past simple is needed: Did many people enter the competition?
c   Again, the competition has finished and the judging has been completed, so the past simple is needed: Who judged the competition?
d   Past simple question forms need the auxiliary 'do' in sentences, like this: How did the judges choose the winner?

    e Question forms like this one need subject/verb inversion: Where are you going to study overseas?

    f The question is about a future arrangement and should therefore be in the present continuous: Are you going overseas next term or not till next year?

    g The question is about 'you' being excited; not about 'I' imagining something, therefore the tag question should be about 'you': I imagine you are excited about going overseas, aren't you?

Homework
1
Descriptions

Photos/drawings

a The roof is thatched.
The walls are made of mud and straw. [photo/drawing of an old English
The windows have small panes of glass.
It's got a pitched roof.

b It's got a flat roof.
It has a balcony.
It's on the third floor of a modern apartment block.
It's made of concrete.

c The roof is made of sheets of metal.
It has a verandah.
It's made of wood.
The windows have small panes of glass.

d It has large picture windows.
There's an integral garage.
It consists of two storeys.
It's got a pitched roof.
It's built of brick.
It has a tiled roof.

e It's got a pitched roof.
It's built of brick.
It has a tiled roof.

f It has a tiled roof.
It's built of brick.
It's got a pitched roof.
The windows have small panes of glass.

g The garage is under the house.
It's built on stilts.
It's got ranch sliders.
It's made of wood.
It has large picture windows.
It has a balcony.

Unit 4
Exercise 3

Sample answers are:

Big differences:
a Peter is much taller than Sue.
b Sue is a good deal fatter than Carole.
c Sue's hair is much darker than Carole's.
Small differences:
a Peter has a little less hair than Darren.
b Sue has slightly less-curly hair than Carole.
c Sue has slightly longer hair than Carole.
d Sue is a little taller than Carole.

Exercise 10

	exactly the same	with regard to X.
	fairly similar	as regards X.
A and B are:	rather different	as far as X is concerned.
	totally different	with respect to X.

Exercise 13   There are many possible answers. Some suggestions are:

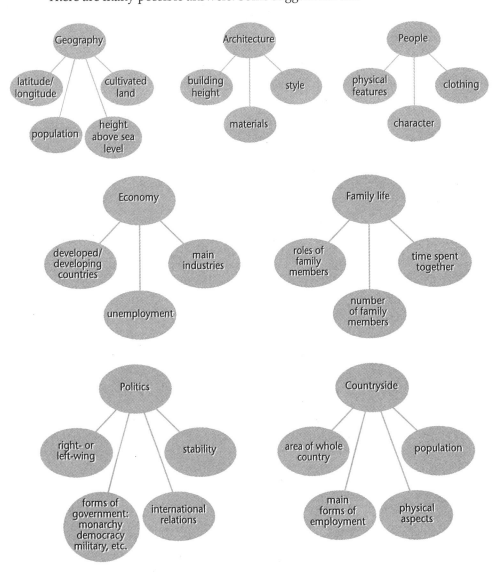

Exercise 15   'My country and New Zealand are totally different with regard to <u>politics</u>. For example, my country has a military <u>government</u>; <u>in contrast</u>, New Zealand has a democratic one.'
Topic – politics
Aspect – government
Comparison/contrast marker – in contrast

'My country and Britain are fairly similar as regards <u>food</u>. For example, <u>as in</u> Britain, <u>so in</u> France the <u>staple food</u> is potatoes.'
Topic – food
Aspect – staple food
Comparison/contrast marker – as in X, so in Y

'My country and Canada are rather different as far as <u>climate</u> is concerned. For example, Canada has four <u>seasons</u> <u>whereas</u> my country has just a wet and a dry <u>season</u>.'
Topic – climate
Aspect – seasons
Comparison/contrast marker – whereas

'My country and Australia are exactly the same with respect to <u>family life</u>. For example, <u>both</u> my country <u>and</u> Australia have a large number of <u>solo parent families</u>.'
Topic – family life
Aspect – solo parent families
Comparison/contrast marker – both X and Y

Exercise 17

Sweden

Age	Institute	Attendance optional or compulsory
5–7	Preschool	optional
8–13	Primary	compulsory
14–16	Lower secondary	compulsory
16–18	Upper secondary	optional

United Kingdom

Age	Institute	Attendance optional or compulsory
2–5	Nursery	optional
5–7	Infants ⎫	
	⎬ Primary	compulsory
8–11	Junior ⎭	
12–16	Secondary	compulsory
16–18	Secondary/sixth form college	optional

Exercise 19

a   The present simple
b   All others
c   People; roles of men and women; your country; education

Unit 5

Exercise 1

Expressing an opinion
From my point of view
As I see it
In my opinion …
It seems to me that
My view is that …
The way I see it …

Expressing preferences
I prefer to …
I'd rather …
I'm more interested in …
… appeals to me more.
I'm more attracted to …
… interests me more.

Expressing likes/dislikes
I enjoy …
I'm keen on …
I'm fond of …
I'm not interested in …
I don't go for …
I'm not into …

Exercise 2

Many students, even at quite high level, do not use more formal opinion expressions than 'I think' even when talking about quite formal topics. This unit encourages you to use suitable formal expressions.

Exercise 3

a	From my point of view	reading is fun.	(sentence)
b	I'd rather	read.	(verb)
c	I'm not particularly interested in	reading.	(gerund)
		books.	(noun)

Exercise 4

They can all be completed with either a noun or a gerund.

Exercise 5

Nouns	**Gerunds**
Heavy metal rock music	listening to heavy metal rock music
	playing heavy metal rock music
Comedy films	watching comedy films
Science fiction books	reading science fiction books
Busy cities	living in busy cities
	visiting busy cities
Sports cars	driving sports cars
	travelling in sports cars
Opera	going to the opera
	listening to opera
	watching opera
Sightseeing	going sightseeing
Horse riding	going horse riding
Competitive sports	playing competitive sports
	watching competitive sports
Team sports	playing team sports
	watching team sports
Spicy food	eating spicy food
Art galleries	going to art galleries
Circuses	going to the circus
Zoos	going to the zoo

Exercise 6

There is more than one possible way of stressing the likes/dislikes expressions, but the following represent fairly common stress patterns:
I en**joy ski**ing.
I'm **keen** on **ski**ing.
I'm **fond** of **ski**ing.
I'm not **interested** in **ski**ing.

I don't **go** for **ski**ing.
I'm not **into** **ski**ing.

Question a

Neutral expressions	Informal expressions
I enjoy …	I don't go for …
I'm keen on …	I'm not into …
I'm fond of …	
I'm not interested in …	

Question b
They would probably use the informal expressions but could also use the neutral expressions.

Question c
He or she would probably use the neutral expressions.

Question d
It depends on the topic you are discussing (is it formal or informal?) and whether the interviewer is talking in a formal or informal way (if he or she is talking to you informally, respond informally; if he or she is talking to you formally, respond more formally).

Exercise 7

I really enjoy skiing; I'm really keen on skiing; I'm really fond of skiing

I enjoy skiing; I'm keen on skiing; I'm fond of skiing

I'm not really interested in skiing; I don't really go for skiing; I'm not really into skiing

I'm not interested in skiing; I don't go for skiing; I'm not into skiing

Exercise 10

a   'that' is pronounced /ðət / (NOT /ðæt/).
b   All the opinion expressions need to be followed by a full sentence with at least a subject and a verb.

Exercise 11

There is more than one possible way of stressing the opinion expressions, but the following represent fairly common stress patterns:
From **my** point of view …
As **I** see it …
In **my** opinion …
It seems to **me** that …
My view is that …
The way **I** see it …

Exercise 14

Her reasons are:
1   She enjoys meeting people.
2   She particularly likes meeting people from different countries.
3   She has a friendly manner.
4   She's very patient.

5 She always likes to look neat and tidy/takes care of her appearance.
6 She speaks three languages.
7 She can type a little.
8 She has a certificate in hospitality and tourism.

Reasons 1–5 are personal qualities
Reasons 6–7 are skills
Reason 8 is a qualification

The opinion expressions that she uses are:
The way I see it,
it seems to me that
(She also uses 'I believe' and 'I feel' as opinion expressions)

Exercise 21

a
I prefer to (+ verb)…
I'd rather (+ verb)…
I'm more interested in (+ noun or gerund)…
…(noun or gerund +) appeals to me more.
I'm more attracted to (+ noun or gerund)…
… (noun or gerund +) interests me more.

b
I pre**fer** to …
I'd **rather** …
I'm **more in**terested in …
… ap**peals** to me more.
I'm **more** attr**ac**ted to …
… **in**terests me more.

c
I much prefer to …
I'd much rather …
I'm much more interested in …
… appeals to me much more.
I'm much more attracted to …
… interests me much more.

Exercise 23

Dialogue 1

Expressing preference:	I'd much rather …
	I prefer reading
Expressing likes/dislikes:	I'm not really into …
Expressing opinion:	the way I see it, …
Giving a reason:	it's really expensive.
Giving a second reason:	another thing is …

Dialogue 2

Expressing preference:	I prefer going …
	watching TV appeals to me much more.
Giving reasons:	the picture is so much bigger and the sound quality is better.
Giving first reason:	For one thing, you can …
Giving a second reason/ expressing a like:	And I enjoy being able to …
Giving another reason:	the main reason is that …

Exercise 25

b
There are many possible answers depending on the situation in different
countries and home cities. Some points to consider are:

cost	speed
safety	health
pollution	comfort
flexibility of route	privacy

Exercise 26

a How do you mean?
b I'm afraid I don't follow you.
c Could you explain what you mean about …?

Exercise 27

The interviewee clarified his ideas by **b** – giving examples

Exercise 28

The exemplification phrases used in the tape are:
For example, X
X is a case in point.
X, for instance.

Other possible phrases include:
X, for example.
An illustration of this is X.
X is an illustration of this.
Take X, for example.
If we look at X …..

Unit 6

Revision exercise a

There are a great many possible answers. Some suggestions are:

Possible benefits
Increased employment opportunities
Improved economy
Overseas currency
Intercultural contact
Market for traditional crafts
Traditional culture maintained
through tourist shows

Possible negative effects
Environmental pollution
Employment only seasonal
Ugly high-rise hotel buildings
Sharp increase in land prices
Local culture changed
Increased crime – wealthy
    tourists robbed

Exercise 1

Honey cake
flour
eggs
milk
honey
sultanas
butter

French onion soup
salt
cheese
onion
garlic
bread
pepper
oil
vegetable stock

Honey cake
beat
cut
mix

French onion soup
slice
fry
stir

stir	sprinkle
pour	boil
bake	simmer
	pour
	grill
	melt

Exercise 2

a The sequence expressions are:

Honey cake	**French onion soup**
At the same time,	while
Then	Then, when
When that's done,	At the same time,
After a while,	When
when	after a few seconds
As soon as that's done,	until
then, immediately,	then
	Meanwhile,
	As soon as
	Immediately after that,
	then
	until

b Present simple

Exercise 5

There are a great number of instruments. Some suggestions are:
piano, guitar, violin, drums, flute, trumpet, saxophone, double bass, cello,
viola, clarinet, harp, electric organ, cymbals, bagpipes, etc.

Exercise 6

The instrument is a guitar.

Information about how the instrument is played – The strings are plucked
with the fingers of one hand. … the strings are pressed down at the far end of
the piece of wood with the fingers of the other hand.
The tense used in the information about how the instrument is played –
present simple passive.
Information about how the instrument is constructed – It consists of a shaped
wooden box with a hole in the middle and a long piece of wood with strings
on.
The sequence expression – At the same time

Exercise 9

left high school
attended a theatre school
worked at a theatre in Liverpool
worked at a theatre in Bristol
was unemployed
worked in a theatre in Norfolk
worked in various theatres
gave up working in the theatre
went to university

Exercise 10

    a   mainly the past simple, but there are also two examples of the present simple and one example of the past perfect.

    b   the text needs more variety of sequence expression; 'then' and 'next' are used too often.

Exercise 12

You could group the expressions in many different ways according to the criteria you use. One grouping would be:

Group 1:
Initially, ...
At first, ...

Group 2: (where there is a time gap between stages)
Subsequently, ...
Later on, ...
Shortly after ...,
Shortly after that, ...
After a while, ...
Some time later, ...
Afterwards, ...

Group 3: (where one stage is immediately followed by the next one)
Then ...
The next stage is/was ...
Having ...,
Next, ...
After that,
After ...,

Group 4:
In the end, ...
Finally, ...

Exercise 13

    a
Subsequently, + sentence
In the end, + sentence
Then + sentence
The next stage is/was + infinitive OR + noun
Initially, + sentence
Finally, + sentence
Later on, + sentence
Having + past participle, + sentence
At first, + sentence
Next, + sentence
After that, + sentence
Shortly after + noun OR + gerund OR + sentence
After + noun OR + gerund, + sentence
Shortly after that, + sentence
After a while, + sentence
Some time later, + sentence
Afterwards, + sentence

Exercise 14

I left school in 1968. I had good examination results and got a place at university but I chose not to take it up. Instead, I went to the Old Vic Theatre School. I spent two years there. In 1970, having graduated from drama school, I initially went to work at the Liverpool Playhouse for a six-month period. Shortly after leaving that job, I got work at the Bristol Repertory Theatre where I spent about three months doing small parts and, after that, I spent about six months 'resting' – the term actors use when they are unemployed. Then I got a job in a summer theatre in Norfolk. At first I did small parts, but later on I was given leading roles to play which was very exciting. Subsequently, I worked in a number of other theatre companies doing a range of acting work. In the end, however, I gave up the theatre and went to university after all. But it had been a really exciting five years of my life.

Exercise 19

It is difficult to decide on an exact rank order, but the suggestions can be divided into good ideas, bad ideas and some that you could use if there is no other possibility:

Good ideas:
c   If you don't know the answer to a question, try to think of an answer while saying something else.
e   If you have no ideas or opinions about a subject, make some tentative guesses and then try to change the subject to something you can talk about.

Possible ideas if you can't follow c or e above:
a   If you don't know the answer to a question, be honest and tell the examiner.

Bad ideas:
d   If you don't know the answer to a question, try to think of an answer by considering the question in silence.
b   If you have no ideas or opinions on a subject, be honest and tell the examiner.
f   If you can't answer a question, tell the examiner that it's a difficult question or that you haven't studied the subject or that you haven't prepared that topic.

Exercise 20

The student in the second text.

Exercise 21

d   If you don't know the answer to a question, try to think of an answer by considering the question in silence.
   • [pause] We eat …
f   If you can't answer a question, tell the examiner that it's a difficult question or that you haven't studied the subject or that you haven't prepared that topic.
   • No, … er… I haven't studied this subject.
c   If you don't know the answer to a question, try to think of an answer while saying something else.
   • Oh, er, that's an interesting question. The main differences?
   • Oh, um, well…well,
   • Um, oh, that's a good question. To be honest, I'm not very sure why there are a lot of unemployed young people, um, but …

e If you have no ideas about a subject, make some tentative guesses and then try to change the subject to something you can talk about.
  - … perhaps one reason could be that our economy has suffered in recent years. Um. Another reason may be that the population has increased and there aren't enough jobs for everyone. As I say, I'm not too sure of the reasons, but it is a serious problem because … well, because of the results.
a If you don't know the answer to a question, be honest and tell the examiner.
  - I don't know.
  - I'm sure there are, but just at the moment I can't think of any.

Exercise 22

a the student comments on the question itself:
  - Oh, that's an interesting question.
  - That's a good question.
b the student uses hesitation devices rather than leave a silence
  - Oh, er, well … Yes, …
  - Um, …
c the student repeats (and may slightly rephrase) the question
  - The main differences?
  - To be honest, I'm not very sure why there are a lot of unemployed young people …

You can, of course, combine any of these strategies together.

Exercise 25

Interviewee:	
Expressing non–comprehension	I'm sorry, I'm afraid I don't understand what you mean.
Using hesitation devices	Oh, er. Well, um …
Sequence expressions	initially; subsequently; after …; shortly after …ing;
Past simple forms	had to; followed; joined; went; decided; took
Past perfect form	had made
Passive form	was offered
Present perfect form	I've worked
Expressing an opinion	In my opinion
Repeating a question	it covers a number of different things; I'm afraid I'm not too sure how much things cost these days.
Comparing and contrasting	a little more dangerous than …
Describing things	It's actually a sort of jacket that you

	can fill with air so that you float on the surface of the water.
Giving reasons	because I bought all my equipment some time ago.
Changing the subject	But scuba diving is such fun that it's worth the money – there's so much to do and see underwater. You can explore wrecks and caves, catch fish and lobster and so on, or just look at the plants and animals that live under water. And underwater photography is very popular too.

Interviewer:

'Wh' questions	How did you train to do that? What does an instructor's course cover? What sort of equipment do you need to go scuba diving?
Tag questions	It's a very dangerous sport, isn't it?
Expressing non–comprehension	Sorry, what does BC mean?
Yes/no questions	Is all this equipment very expensive?

Exercise 26

The activities are:
a photography
b tennis
c playing the piano
d skiing
e swimming
f cooking

Unit 7
Revision exercise 2

a the revision exercise is intended primarily to revise:
  • the use of sequence expressions
  • the use of strategies to cope with difficult questions (e.g. using hesitation devices, changing the topic, commenting on the question, repeating the question)

but could also have been useful to revise:
  • responding to information
  • dealing with vocabulary problems (expressing non-comprehension, explaining unknown words)
  • asking for repetition
  • expressing opinions
  • comparing and contrasting
  • asking for clarification of ideas
  • clarifying ideas

Exercise 4

Group A

a job	a position
a **field** of **study**	a **subject**
certain	**defin**ite
to **plan** on	to in**tend** to
an oppor**tu**nity	a chance
a firm	a **com**pany
an aim	a goal
initial	first
a need	a de**mand**

to plan on + noun or gerund
to intend to + verb

Group B

initially (adv)	at first
ultimately (adv)	in the end
ideally (adv)	best of all
rapidly	fast
be**lie**ve (v)	think
com**plete** (v)	finish
an**ti**cipate (v)	expect
hope (v)	would like
post (n)	job
carry out (v)	do

In general, the left-hand column of vocabulary is more suitable for a formal conversation about future plans.

1	**a** and **b** are both possible.	4	**b** is correct.
2	**a** and **b** are both possible.	5	**a** is correct.
3	**a** is correct.		

Exercise 6

Dialogue 1

Weak points
- The language is inadequate (the sentences are very short and simple; the vocabulary is very basic; the language is rather informal).
- The ideas are limited and do not suggest mature thought.

Good point
- The length of the responses is fair (but could be longer).

Dialogue 2

Weak points
- The responses are far too short and therefore contain very little information.

Good point
- The language is at the right level of formality.

Exercise 7

Interviewer: According to your CV, you're going to study hospitality and tourism. Why have you chosen that particular subject?

Student: **GIVES REASON (OPINION): I believe a qualification in hospitality and tourism will provide me with the necessary skills for a job in the hotel industry.**
PROVIDES SUPPORT FOR OPINION: (f) The tourist industry

in my country is growing rapidly and there is a real demand for people with such a qualification.
GIVES A SECOND REASON: (c) Another reason is that I enjoy meeting people and making contact with people from overseas, so I feel that I'm well suited to working in the field of hospitality and tourism.

Interviewer: I see. And what will you do after you complete your hospitality and tourism course?

Student: OUTLINES FUTURE WORK PLANS: I intend to return home and I'll probably apply for a position with an international chain of hotels.
GIVES AN EXAMPLE: (e) such as the Hilton Group.
GIVES FURTHER DETAILS OF FUTURE WORK PLANS: (a) Initially, I anticipate working as a hotel receptionist, but I hope to work my way up into hotel management.

Interviewer: And what is your ambition?

Student: STATES AMBITION: Ultimately, I plan on becoming a hotel manager.
GIVES DETAILS OF AMBITION: (d) Ideally, I'd like to work in a hotel in an English-speaking country. PROVIDES REASONS: (b) because, in my opinion, living and working in another culture is very stimulating, and also because I'd like to use my English language skills.

Exercise 8

Interviewer: On your CV, you state that you're applying for a course in accountancy. Why have you chosen that particular field of study?

Student: GIVES A REASON FOR SUBJECT CHOICE: (b) It's a subject that I've always enjoyed and as a high school student I did well in it.
GIVES A SECOND REASON: (g) Also, I believe that there are good job opportunities for people with accountancy qualifications.

Interviewer: I see. And what exactly will you do after you complete your accountancy course?

Student: OUTLINES POSSIBLE FUTURE WORK PLAN: (a) I have no definite plans at the moment, but I expect I'll start by applying for a junior post in the accounts department of a large organisation;
GIVES AN EXAMPLE: (f) an international company, for instance.
GIVES REASONS FOR WORK PLAN: (c) In addition to providing me with initial work experience, it would give me the opportunity to see the range of work that a large accounts department carries out.

Interviewer: And what is your ambition?

Student: STATES AMBITION: (e) My ultimate ambition is to have my own successful accountancy firm. It is, of course, a long-term goal but
GIVES A REASON FOR AMBITION: (d) I believe that I'd prefer to be my own boss rather than work for someone else.

Exercise 16

After completing	having completed; on completing; when I have completed; after I have completed
intend to return	plan on returning; expect to return; anticipate returning
may	might; could
post	position; job
Alternatively	or; on the other hand; as an alternative
could	might; may
firm	company; business
option	alternative; possibility; potential; choice
position	post
company	firm; business
On the other hand	alternatively; as an alternative; or
might	may; could
aim	goal; ambition

Exercise 18

Expressing desire to do something
A **dream** of mine is to …
My **dream** is to …
I'd **love** to …
I'd **really** like to …
I have a **real** de**sire** to …

Expressing interest in something
I'm **fasc**inated by …
I'm **really interested** in …
I find X **really interesting**.
I think X is **ab**solutely **fasc**inating
I'm in**trig**ued by …
X **really** ap**peals** to me.

All the 'desire' expressions can be followed by a verb. All the 'interest' expressions would incorporate a noun (or noun phrase) or a gerund.

Exercise 19

Possible notes:
Ambitions
1   Visit Lhasa – capital of Tibet c. 3500 m in Himalayas. See monasteries and pilgrims.
2   Speak Samoan fluently – (speak 3 langs.) Samoan accent attractive.

Exercise 20

The student uses all the functions twice:
Personal ambitions? Well, yes, I suppose I do, actually. OUTLINES AN AMBITION: I'd really like to visit Lhasa – you know, the capital of Tibet. GIVES DETAILS OF AN AMBITION: It's about 3500 metres high, up in the Himalayan mountains. GIVES REASONS FOR AN AMBITION: I'm fascinated by Tibet and by the Tibetan Buddhist religion and I'd love to see the monasteries in Lhasa, and the Tibetan pilgrims who go there. OUTLINES AN AMBITION: And another ambition of mine is to speak Samoan fluently. GIVES REASONS FOR AN AMBITION: I'm really interested in learning languages – I can speak three quite well – and there's something particularly beautiful about the sound of the Samoan language – I find the Samoan accent really attractive. GIVES DETAILS OF AN AMBITION: So I'd love to be able to speak it well, you know, and with a good accent.

Unit 8

Revision exercise b

The aim of revision exercise **a** was for you to use the language and functions presented in Unit 7 – Expressing hopes and plans; Giving reasons; Expressing alternatives; Expressing desire and interest.

Exercise 2

They are all grammatically correct.

Exercise 3

a Student A is expressing an 'unreal' possibility – he thinks it is very unlikely (or even impossible) that he will get 4.5 on the IELTS test. In contrast, Student B is expressing a possibility for the future that he sees as having a real chance of occurring – he thinks it is possible that he will get 4.5 in the IELTS test.

b This structure is often called the second conditional. It's form is:
If + ... past simple ...., I + ...would + infinitive ......

c This structure is often called the first conditional. It's form is:
If + ... present simple ...., I + ...will + infinitive ....

Exercise 5

Student A is expressing what he thinks are 'real possibilities' for the future.

Exercise 6

Student B is expressing what he thinks are 'unreal' hypotheses about the future.

Exercises 8 and 9

Uncertainty
I'm not too **sure** what/who/where/when/how/why ...
I'm not entirely **sure**.
I'm not altogether **cer**tain.
It's **difficult** to **say** what/who/where/when/how/why ...
It's **difficult** to **know** what/who/where/when/how/why ...
It re**mains** to be **seen** what/who/where/when/how/why ...

Supposition
I i**mag**ine ...
I guess ...
I sus**pect** ...
I sup**pose** ...

Possibility
I may ...
I could ...
I might ...
Per**haps** ...
Maybe .....
It's **pos**sible that .....

Exercise 11

Possible notes:

Problems
A no. of problems – academic + social
Biggest – getting to know people/making friends.

a overseas students – make friends at International Student Club
b local students/native Eng. speakers – difficult to make friends?

Reasons
a language barrier   - informal colloquial Eng. for socialising
                                  - different Eng. accents
b cultural gap

Exercise 12

Solutions
a end of lecture/tutorial – talk about course work to break the ice
b go for a cup of tea/coffee – chat. But how to continue?
c join a club – talk about shared interest

Exercise 17

I suppose; I'm not altogether certain; I imagine; it remains to be seen; perhaps; I may; I suspect; I'm not sure; I may; I'm not entirely sure; I guess; maybe; I could; it's difficult to know how; I suppose.

The functions/skills are: Asking questions; Greeting and introducing yourself; Saying goodbye; Describing things/giving general information; Expressing non–comprehension; Explaining unknown words; Asking for repetition; Responding to information; Comparing; Contrasting; Expressing likes and dislikes; Expressing opinions; Expressing preferences; Giving reasons; Asking for clarification of ideas; Clarifying ideas; Describing a sequence of events; Changing the topic; Using hesitation devices; Commenting on the question; Repeating the question; Expressing plans; Expressing hopes and ambitions; Expressing alternatives; Expressing desire; Expressing interest; Hypothesising; Expressing uncertainty; Expressing possibility; Expressing supposition.